SOLDIERS

AND THEIR

BATTLE
DRILLS

SOLDIERS

AND THEIR

BATTLE DRILLS

SPIRITUAL WARFARE

QUOTED FROM - INFANTRYMAN'S CREED - "IF NECESSARY, I WILL FIGHT TO MY DEATH..."
BIBLICAL PARALLEL "FOR ME, LIVING IS CHRIST DYING IS GAIN" (PHILIPPIANS 1:21)

PASTOR JESSE POSNER

XULON ELITE

Xulon Press Elite
2301 Lucien Way #415
Maitland, FL 32751
407.339.4217
www.xulonpress.com

Unless otherwise indicated, Scripture quotations taken from the Holman Christian Standard Bible (HCSB). Copyright © 1999, 2000, 2002, 2003, 2009 by Holman Bible Publishers, Nashville Tennessee. All rights reserved.

Paperback ISBN-13: 978-1-66285-239-8
Ebook ISBN-13: 978-1-66285-240-4

Table of Contents

Chapter 1

WHY BATTLE DRILLS

When looking into our spiritual walk, and how we should react to everyday life, to everyday attacks of the enemy. I have come to realize that my training in the military is very relevant. During my 13 years in the United States Army, I have learned many tactics, drills, and methods to keep not only myself alive in conflict, but also my battle buddy (fellow Soldier). To be successful in combat, you must train to win. We have a saying in the Army, "Train how you fight". This was to ensure we kept training practical and to the point. Battle Drills not only describe how Soldiers in a Platoon or Squad maneuver in commonly encountered situations in a combat zone, but they also allow the soldier and/or leader to make decisions rapidly and with little thought. Battle Drills were meant to be practiced repeatedly, so that they become muscle memory. Think about it. When someone swings at you, or if something that will hurt is flying toward you, a natural reaction occurs. You put up your arms to block, or you go to duck, or you turn away and close your eyes. Whatever the reaction, this is a natural one that occurs without much thought, sometimes no thought at all.

This is the goal for any Platoon leader or Squad leader with their Soldiers when practicing Battle Drills. The hope is to train on these eight (8) basic drills so much so, the soldiers all react as if it is their bodies natural response to the situation. The Military definition of a Battle Drill is "a collective action rapidly executed without applying a deliberate decision-making process" (25-101, 2022). Why am I explaining what a Battle Drill is you may be thinking? Well, one morning during my quiet time with God, I was meditating on the scripture that speaks on spiritual warfare and how the battle is raging all around us. I was looking at Ephesians 6:10-20, seeing how our battle is not with *"flesh and blood, but against the rulers, against the authorities, against the world powers of this darkness…"* (v.12 HCSB). I realized, not only do we have all the equipment needed for battle, but we also have all we need to be prepared for any attack or threat. We can actually bring the fight to the enemy with all we are blessed with through God's mercies, and the gift of Jesus Christ! Nonetheless, it caused me to wonder, what am I doing in my life today that is living this truth out? It troubled me, as the answer was…" not so much". I was not prepared for the enemy. I was taking the tools and training available to me through the revelation of God (The Bible) for granted. I started asking myself hard questions at this point. How could I turn this around? How could I not only grow in my relationship with God, and in my walk with Christ, but also go on the offensives? In what way, with the guidance of the Holy Spirit and strength Christ gives me, takeout enemy strongholds?

I also came to realize that we do not give much thought on the reality of the battle raging on around us. We are told we are in a spiritual battle; however, we live as if we are at peace. Now don't get me wrong, when you have Jesus Christ as Lord and Savior you are living in peace with God, but the battle on earth for the souls of mankind rages on. You can see the difference in how people live in a country that has known combat for many years, as those in Afghanistan and Iraq. You see a big difference in what they do on a daily basis. All their actions have purpose for the most part, they do not do much that does not have an end goal in mind. They live life in the ready, not in fear, and not as if all is peachy. They live life in a state of "possibly" … possibly something could happen so I need to be ready, prepared and trained for whatever could occur. For the majority of America, and this includes the Church. We have gotten complacent and live as if nothing could ever happen. This is exactly what the enemy in combat looks for (complacency) prior to attack, and there is no difference with the enemy of God's people. 1 John 1:8 says, "*If we say, "We have no sin," we are deceiving ourselves, and the truth is not in us.*" This is what the devil is waiting for, waiting to pounce on; all he is looking for is a foot hold.

That is when it hit me like a ton of bricks. God showed me that He not only gave me all the material (Bible), but

He also allowed me to go into a profession that taught a simple type of repetition that created a type of muscle memory when it came to warfare: BATTLE DRILLS; "they provide for a smooth transition from one activity to another. For example, from movement to offensive action to defensive action" (25-101, 2022). It was then that I thought that I could prepare spiritually as I did in the Military. By putting this type of training into action with my spiritual life, I would not only spend more time with God on a daily basis, but I would also turn my spiritual disciplines, defenses, and attacks into muscle memory. Every day we are faced with attacks, tricks, and temptations. We cannot think that just because we are part of God's family the trials go away as some may believe. Or take it to the other extreme, that there is no obligation to surrender our thoughts over to God, or the way we live life and act is of little consequence to the Kingdom of God.

Every day we must surrender to God, pick up our cross, and follow Him. By doing so, it will enable us to defend against the trials and temptations the enemy will throw at us in life. Trials and temptations that some may think are big, and some may think are small. Either way, it is what the enemy uses to get a foothold. For example, feeling the need to lie regarding remedial things like when you are asked, "does this outfit makes me look fat?" To cheating on your spouse; not excluding neglecting your family for your job or ministry. The attacks come in all different ways, shapes, and forms. The question is, will we be prepared for it when it comes? Will we be able to recognize the attack and smoothly transition from one activity to another, from normal day activity to offensive action to defensive action as if it were muscle memory?

The material in this book is not meant to answer all problems, and it is defiantly not going to work 100% of the time. We have the Bible, God's mercy and grace, and the sacrifice of Jesus Christ that trumps anything I could ever come up with. Jesus Christ is the answer, He is the way, the truth, and the life. We must live a life that is dependent on Him, one that allows Him to guide us. My hope for this book is to encourage, equip, and prepare the Saints for battle. To show that God has given us all we need. All we must do is, trust God, use what He has provided us with, and live it out!

Questions for thought:

1. Why is it so easy to turn back to our old-self ways?

2. Why do we put so much effort into learning and training for things of this world, but when it comes to God, the one we say is our Lord, we are ok with spending little to no time with Him?

Chapter 2

CONDUCT PLATOON ATTACK

Evangelism

Military Explanation:

T his battle drill is used when the leader of the Team, Squad, or Platoon plans what their group will do when contact is initiated with the enemy. This one is considered an offensive battle drill, as it explains that the team, squad, or platoon is to be the one that initiates the contact; it is a deliberate attack on the enemy. A plan must be made, briefed, and understood prior to the execution and initiation of the contact. There are two steps in this battle drill that involve positioning and support elements. Of course, identifying who and where the enemy is located is vital. The main idea is based off what to do if your team is not detected, and how to begin if you are detected by the enemy. If you are detected, you would start the battle by initiating battle drill #2, but we will get to that one in the next chapter.

Conditions for this battle drill involve the enemy having an occupied position/s, or the enemy is moving in front of your unit. The group that is conducting the battle drill is attacking as a small group, or a part of a larger one. The main points and objectives of this battle drill is the fact that the group is not surprised or fixed by the enemy. The plan, or reason of attack is accomplished by capturing, destroying, or causing the enemy to withdraw. Part of the plan that cannot be overlooked is, the unit must also accomplish the attack with enough of a force to defeat any counterattack and to continue the main operation/mission (25-101, 2022).

Biblical Parallel:

Since the Fall of Mankind in the Garden, Mankind has had an enemy. This enemy made the first move, was the first to attack (Genesis 3). The enemy thought for a long time that he had won. He created a situation where all of us (Humans) have a sinful nature due to the fall we read about in Genesis. So, knowing there is an enemy, we must learn not only how to protect ourselves, but also how we can go on the offensive. The battle drill requires that we know where the enemy is, along with other intel on how they operate, who they are, etc. This is outlined for us in the bible (the brief so to speak). We are told in

Isaiah 14:12-15 how Satan (our adversary), was thrown out of Heaven. Then we see from passages like 1 John 5:19 that tell us, "We know that we are from God, and the *whole world lies in the power of the evil one.* (Italicized for point)" The world we live in is the territory of the Devil and his followers, and those that would choose the desires of the flesh above God.

We know the tactics of the enemy. We are warned in how he is traveling around, "prowls around like a roaring lion, seeking someone to devour" (1 Peter 5:8). The type of fighting he does can be summed up in John 8:44, when Jesus was responding to the religious leaders of the time, pointing out how they have lost their way; (they are aiding and abiding the enemy). This passage states, *"You are of your father the Devil, and you want to carry out your father's desires. He was a murderer from the beginning and has not stood in the truth, because there is no truth in him. When he tells a lie, he speaks from his own nature, because he is a liar and the father of liars".* We know who our enemy is, and we know how he works. This is how we can properly put this battle drill into practice. The only difference here is we do not destroy or condemn the devil's soldiers (people that are lost), we attack in a way that will set them free. We attack in a way that shows them God's love, and how they too can become members of this Family of God!

Our Marching Orders:

We have very specific orders when it comes to how we go on the offensive with the enemy. It is to bring the Gospel to those that are lost. We are to bring the message of Jesus Christ, and Him crucified and raised on our behalf to the ranks of the enemy. We must be ready, trained and proficient in the Will of God, and to wholly trust the Holy Spirit to give us the tools and words needed to be successful when we engage in "Platoon Attack" … or what I like to call it and many others, "Evangelism". Not only are we told that the people of God were to be a "Blessing" to all the nations (Gen. 12:2-3), but it is reiterated when Christ finishes His work on the Cross. It is known as the "Great Commission" (Matt. 28:16-20). There is no questioned about it, we have been given the order to move forward with our "Platoon Attack". We do not need to wait for further instructions, as how to do it, and what to say is all summed up in the Bible.

We have example after example of the Apostles, and other followers of Jesus on how this is done. We have example after example of what not to do in the Old and New Testament. We are shown that we are to do it in Love (1 Cor 13.; 1 John 4:7-8; 1 Peter 4:8). We are asked to do it in a gentle way, but boldly (Acts 28:31; 1 Peter 3:15). Overall, when the talk seems cheap, we are expected to preach and share the Gospel of Jesus Christ to those that are lost in how we live (Matt. 5:16; Micah 6:8). There is no question about it, we are told to "Go", and we are expected to be God's hands and feet in this lost and hurting world. To be capable in this we must know God's Will for our lives to move forward with our Attack. The only way to know Him is to pray, to read His Word, and to put it into practice. It's not enough to know the order and names of the books of the Bible, or to have knowledge of what is written in it. We must do something with it, we must put it into action, be "Doers of the Word" as James puts it (James 1:22).

This is sharing the gospel with a neighbor, or friend, or family member. It is repaying evil with good; it is forgiving those that hurt you, it is praying for those that hate you and persecute you. Every day we must be ready and looking for those we can bring the Gospel of Jesus Christ to. During a "Platoon Attack" the soldiers are intentionally looking for the enemy, and their strongholds. These strongholds are not hard to find, they are all around us, and could even be in a place you would think it could never be (Churches, schools, businesses, recreation places, etc.) Every day we must make the decision to carry out the orders to attack the enemy where it hurts, and it hurts the enemy the most when we bring Salvation to those who are lost. The enemy does not want us to make any ground, but when we bring more to the saving knowledge of Christ, we move the Kingdom forward!

Train How you Fight: *Here we will point out practical ways you can practice/train, so we can attempt to make these Spiritual Disciplines muscle memory.*

You may be thinking that this sounds great, but how are we to "train" to do this? Well, you are in luck because, I will share a few ways we can. There are many things you can do to become more comfortable in Platoon Attack/ Evangelism. First, this is a type of evangelism that is done with more than one person, hence the word "Platoon", however, it can be practiced as one also. Keep this in mind however, it will be easier to do when you are not alone. Ecclesiastes 4:11-13 (HCSB), *"Also, if two lie down together, they can keep warm; but how can one person alone keep warm? And if someone overpowers one person, two can resist him. A cord of three strands is not easily broken. Better is a poor but wise youth than an old but foolish king who no longer pays attention to warnings.* Platoon attack is effective because there is strength and accountability in numbers.

You can look up common asked questions/issues that people have with religion, faith, or Christianity. Then you can find answers to these questions by reading the Bible, looking through Commentaries, or Christian apologetic websites and books. Just off the top of my head, here are a few sites you can go to for free information.

- https://answersingenesis.org/ (Answers in Genesis is a great site with information for all types of questions).

- https://www.equip.org/ (The Christian Research Institute is also a good one. Here you can also email their staff with questions. They will then email you the answer with additional reading material).

- https://bibleproject.com/ (The Bible Project. They too have an enormous amount of material you can use to better understand subjects, and easy ways to share it).

These are but a few you can find online. There are many more, and there are many, many books out there by great authors that can help. This is how you can prepare. You should practice this with a friend. Then, you practice answering these questions in your own words, and having follow up questions being asked to you from the person you are practicing with. This way the friend can give rebuttals, follow up questions, and discussion. As if he is the real person you are sharing with. The only way to be comfortable in speaking with someone you do not know, or someone you know just a little of, is by practice. Just like you would do in a public speaking course. In public speaking you give speeches to the class, and each time you do so, you get better and better. But most of all, we must rely on the Holy Spirit. This is key, this is where you will get your boldness, your wisdom, and the words to say. We are told in Luke 12:11-12, *"So you can anticipate that you will be put on trial before the synagogues and religious officials. Don't worry how you'll respond, and don't worry what you should say. The Holy Spirit will give you the words to say at the moment when you need them."* Relying on God is key in any "Platoon Attack", just like relying on your platoon leader and the information they gave you is essential in combat.

Questions for thought:

1. Why do many believers shy away from going on the offensive when it comes to the Kingdom of God? Do they feel like they will offend someone? And if so, why is it so easy to share other things?

2. How can we overcome some of the issues we have discussed from question 1?

3. Do you agree we should "train how we fight"? Why or why not?

Chapter 3

REACT TO CONTACT

Temptation

Military Explanation:

React to Contact is the most common Battle Drill we learn in the Military. Why, because it is one of the most common situations a soldier will find themselves in when doing patrols, guard duty, or convoys. It is when a platoon, either halted or moving, is attacked by the enemy. The platoon was attacked by an unknown or known enemy in the area. The platoon or unit of soldiers return fire immediately. At this time the Team Leader or Squad Leader will start to give commands to the group/unit to gain fire superiority. This is when we have the upper hand in regard to rate of fire, casualties, and moveability. This is also when the leader will have the Unit begin to flank or move forward on the enemy, and/or out of the engagement area. The goal of this battle drill is to take or destroy the enemy who initiated the attack, and to regroup, check supplies, and the wellbeing of the soldiers in your unit.

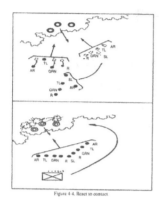

R = Rifleman   GRN = Grenadier

TL = Team Lead   SL = Squad Lead

AR = Automatic Riflemen

Figure 4-4. React to contact

If the unit is unable to gain fire superiority, and cannot take the enemy that started the attack, then the unit must "Break Contact". This is the third battle drill and will be covered in the next Chapter. React to Contact is best described as the entry way too many other Battle Drills. I say this because, it all depends on what is happening, how many enemy soldiers there are, what kind of equipment they have, and how much of all those same things just mentioned you currently have. This will determine what you are to do after starting the Battle Drill, "React to Contact". As stated above, it could very well turn into Battle Drill three if things do not go well, and you could go into full on assault, turning it into Battle Drill one, and so forth. That being said, this is something all soldiers should take seriously, as it could turn the tides for them in a good or bad way in an instant (25-101, 2022).

Biblical Parallel:

This Battle Drill has a strong Biblical parallel and is discussed in many different areas of the Bible. To sum it all up in a sentence, this is when we are faced with temptation of any kind out of nowhere. Just like the battle drill, you could have known the enemy was there or would attack, or you did not see them coming. Either way, contact was made in the form of temptation, and it is now your turn to respond/react to it. The Bible is full of examples of Leaders in the faith, small and large, great or mediocre, dealing with contact with the enemy (Temptation). How it goes all depends on how well you have prepared, what you know, the resources you have, and who you have with you. We have a great example of how to combat/react to contact from Jesus when He was tempted in the Wilderness. In Matthew 4:1-11, we see that the enemy attacks. Satan comes to Jesus while He is out in the wilderness to tempt Him (attack Him).

Right when the enemy opened fire so to speak, Jesus was ready to return fire. Satan tempts Christ with hunger (desires of the flesh). Jesus fires back with the Word of God, stating scripture, letting the enemy know that we do not survive on food alone, but from every Word that comes from the mouth of God (Matt. 4:4). The next two times the enemy attacks, Christ attacks back with more Scripture. At one point, the enemy tries to use Scripture against Jesus by misquoting/taking it out of context. Jesus knew this, did not waver, and was able to continue His react to contact. In the end, Jesus caused the Devil to flee. As we can see, this situation was a successful "React to Contact" battle. Just like the battle drill described above could have many possible outcomes depending on how you handle it, for Humanity, temptation could have a few different consequences as well.

The enemy is real and is waiting and wanting to attack (1 Peter 5:8; John 10:10; Ephesians 6:11). He is out there, and his tactic is to tempt us with all types of things that are contrary to God and His plan. How we react will show how prepared we were for this imminent attack. Will we resist, or will we give in? Will we know what to do, or will we be caught off guard? Will we have the proper "weapons" to return fire and push through, or will we be over ran? Will we know who to rely on and receive our orders from, or will we rely souly on ourselves and what the World says? These are questions we must ask ourselves when it comes to being prepared to react to contact. We ask these questions in physical combat, or forms of these questions in business, and relationships. Why would we not understand and prepare like this for our spiritual walk?

Our Marching Orders:

Again, just like the first Battle Drill, we have specific orders on how to deal with this. On how to conduct our "React to Contact". We are told how we are to act toward those in the World, both lost and saved. The Bible also speaks on how to deal with temptation, and how we can trust in God when temptation comes our way. These scriptures are our "Marching Orders" for this Battle Drill. First, do not be overwhelmed or feel it is hopeless when caught in the crossfire of temptation, for we are told in 1 Corinthians 10:13, *"No temptation has overtaken you except what is common to humanity. God is faithful, and He will not allow you to be tempted beyond what you are able, but with the temptation He will also provide a way of escape so that you are able to bear it."* This passage is bringing hope to God's people when under attack, telling us that God is there with a way of escape. This could be "escape" to move into "Break Contact" (which we will discuss next chapter). Or it could mean a way to go on the offensive and take the enemy. It all depends on your walk and maturity in Christ, but the truth to hold on to is God is there with you.

Second, we are told to stay in communication with "Headquarters". Matthew 26:41 says, *"Stay awake and pray, so that you won't enter into temptation. The spirit is willing, but the flesh is weak."* This passage is Jesus speaking to His disciples while He was on Gethsemane, waiting to be handed over to be crucified. He understood that because of our sin nature, even with our good intentions, we could not do this on our own. We cannot fight temptation solo, we need God with us, we need the covering of Christ. Our orders here are to be on guard, watchful, and in all situations ask for God's strength to fight temptation. This part ties into the first, we need God with us, and we need to be in communication with Him to fight.

Third, we need to know the "OPORD" (Operations Order), the document that gives us essential information so we can understand the situations we are in and will face… the Bible! We see in Matthew chapter 4, Jesus using Scripture to combat temptation. At one point starting in verse 5, the Devil also uses scripture out of context to trick Jesus with the temptation. However, since Jesus knew His Scripture, He was able to defend with Scripture pointing out the flaw in what the Devil said. This is very important. If we do not know the Word of God, it can be used as ammunition against us. We must study, read, meditate on, and prayerfully apply the Word of God to our lives with the help of the Holy Spirit. This is just as important to our walk as it is for a soldier leading troops into battle. The Word of God tells us what to do, what not to do, and ways to do it.

Lastly, you are always better off with a "Battle Buddy" as we call it in the Military. Someone to watch your back, someone to hold you accountable, to fight alongside you. As stated earlier in the book, Ecclesiastes 4:11-13 speaks on how we are stronger together. How it is harder to break a cord of two or three. This is important in everything we are talking about here, and what we will speak of in the next chapters. We always need Christ (one Cord), with us (two cords), and a Battle Buddy (three cords). This is how we will be the strongest when combating temptation (React to Contact).

Train How you Fight: *Here we will point out practical ways you can practice/train, so we can attempt to make these Spiritual Disciplines muscle memory.*

"This is all good, and sounds great" you may be saying, "but how do we put this type of situation into practice?" There are a few ways you could practice this and be ready for the attack. A great way to put this into practice is to have a small group, or at least a close trusted friend that you meet with once a week in person or over the phone/internet with. This group or friend is where you can grow in your walk with Christ together and keep each other accountable. You can share what you have been struggling with, what you have failed in, and what you have succeeded in during the past week. This way you both know what is going on with each other and can call to check in on each other if you know there is a current, and real struggle going on with temptation. This is how many Soldiers struggling with suicide and depression hold each other accountable and keep each other safe.

Another way to put this into practice is to have a documented plan, like a "Fire Drill". This may sound like a waste of time, or it may sound like we are overdoing it, but it works. If it did not work, we would not create fire drills for fires, and have our children practice them a few times a year. All that needs to be done is to write down the following;

1. Begin to pray and ask God for help. Have a passage from the Bible that you will recite, pray on, and keep in mind as you go through the next steps.

2. <u>Who</u> you would call when you feel overwhelmed with temptation, whatever it may be.

3. <u>What</u> you should do if you are feeling overwhelmed with temptation and you are alone, and/or you cannot get ahold of your "Battle Buddy". For example, leave the area or place of temptation, have a backup to call, go directly to your Church, etc.

4. <u>Where</u>, plan/designate spots you can meet your "Battle Buddy" or places you can go that distract you from the overwhelming temptation. A place you can pray and be with God.

I have this type of plan. I have had it for such a long time now that I have it memorized, and it is what you would call muscle memory. The passage I recite and pray on as I talk to God is from Hebrews. Hebrews 10:19-25 (HCSB),

> *"19 Therefore, brothers, since we have boldness to enter the sanctuary through the blood of Jesus, 20 by a new and living way He has opened for us through the curtain (that is, His flesh), 21 and since we have a great high priest over the house of God, 22 let us draw near with a true heart in full assurance of faith, our hearts sprinkled clean from an evil conscience and our bodies washed in pure water. 23 Let us hold on to the confession of our hope without wavering, for He who promised is faithful. 24 And let us be concerned about one another in order to promote love and good works, 25 not staying away from our worship meetings, as some habitually do, but encouraging each other, and all the more as you see the day drawing near.*

I have two people I can call, and I have three different places I am able to go if I must get away in a time of overwhelming temptation if I cannot get ahold of my "Battle Buddies". It has helped me many times, and once it becomes muscle memory you won't even think twice about it. You will react as if it is the natural response to temptation when it attempts to creep in. The most important part, however, is the prayer. We must always go to God first! We lean on Him, we trust in Him, we follow Him and no one and nothing else!

Questions for thought:

1. Read James 1:13-15.

   a. Have you ever thought, "why is God putting this temptation in my way?" Or "Satan is the reason I did that?"

2. Why do we always want put place blame instead of combating the temptation?

   a. Read 1 Cor. 10:13 and 1 John 1:5; 4:8-10. What do these passages say to you regarding temptation and God's role in your life?

3. What are some temptations you battle frequently? After reading this chapter, what are some ways you could "React To Contact"?

Chapter 4

BREAK CONTACT

Know when to Flee

Military Explanation:

B reak Contact is a battle drill that a group, squad, or platoon may use (mounted or dismounted), when all parts of the unit is receiving fire/contact from the enemy. When the amount of force, size, or surprise the enemy has on the unit, will determine if the Leader will order "Break Contact". The team will usually conduct the same maneuvering as you would see in React to Contact. They would get down and find adequate cover in order to return fire, and do what they call "fire and move". The team leader would tell each team/group to move at different times, while the other team/group is giving cover/suppressive fire. Then, once that team/group gets to the location they maneuvered to, they would get down and give suppressive fire. This way the other team/group can get up and maneuver to a new location. This would continue until they arrived at the designated rally point, which is out of the "Kill Zone/area of contact".

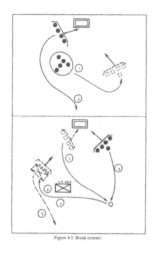

Figure 4-5. Break contact.

R = Rifleman   GRN = Grenadier

TL = Team Lead   SL = Squad Lead

AR = Automatic Riflemen

Then the leader would check on his/her soldiers, give his/her leadership a report of the situation, reorganize as necessary, and continue the mission. There are some other details given if they get split up, or if the Rally point is not safe, however, I will not go into that for this chapter. It is good to understand that in all circumstances, we must be flexible, and have an idea of what to do if our first plan does not pan out. This could involve calling in air support, additional soldiers, or even to change course and push through the enemy (React to Contact). This is all decided upon by the leaders assessment of the situation, strengths, weaknesses, and resources of the team and terrain when contact is initiated. I feel that this battle drill involves a leader to have more strength in his/her character than any other Battle Drill. I say this because, this is when the leader must know their own limitations, as well as his team's. The leader must be able to swallow his/her pride to "walk away" and know when to fight another day. This will ensure the team can regroup, and complete the overall mission put forth by their Commander at a later time. (25-101, 2022).

Biblical Parallel:

In the Bible there are many situations and passages telling us to resist/to flee the enemy, the devil, and our own evil desires. 1 Cor. 6:18 tells us to *Run/or flee* from sexual immorality. Also, in 1 Cor. 10:14 we are told to *flee* from idolatry. Paul writes to Timothy in 1 Timothy 6:9-11 to flee temptation for material things above God, such as money. In 2 Timothy 2:22 Paul warns Timothy about the dangers of youthful passions, self-indulgence, and selfish ambition and to flee from such things. Paul is pointing out to Timothy, and to all who read these letters, that there is a time to run. There is a time when it will be too much for us to handle in that moment, and we must be ready to flee the scene, to regroup, and consult our God on what to do. Because in all these passages it does not end with, just fleeing. It ends with the pursuit of God, His righteousness, and what is of God. They explain that we must seek Him (God) (1 Tim. 6:13). Seek God's glory and His will (1 Cor. 10:31-33).

We see champions of the faith running from situations that seemed too big for them in the moment. Champions such as Joseph, who ran from Potiphar's Wife in Genesis 39. He attempted to refuse her sexual offer (reacted to contact), but then soon realized the enemy had the advantage, so he broke contact (Gen 39:11-13). We are even told in the Word of God that, God Himself is assisting us in this type of situation. In 1 Corinthians 10:13 it says, "*No temptation has overtaken you except what is common to humanity. God is faithful, and He will not allow you to be tempted beyond what you are able, but with the temptation <u>He will also provide a way of escape so that you are able to bear it</u>.*" This is very encouraging, but it tells us that we have no excuse when it comes to falling into temptation. God is there, giving us a way to "Break Contact" if you will, when we are faced with something overwhelming that is contrary to the righteousness of God.

**We must remember that even when we must flee the enemy, this is not a defeat. This is a victory and portrayed as such in the Word of God. Why? Because you have been faithful, humble, obedient to God, and you did not sin! The enemy wants you to sin, and when you resist, or flee, and do not sin, you have won because of the power of God that is in you through Jesus Christ.

Our Marching Orders:

Our Marching orders are simple. I have alluded to them in the section above; it is to know when to run/flee. We need to be honest with ourselves, and know when we cannot resist, and we must leave the situation, the scene. God knows that we are bent toward sin, and we have trouble saying no to our temptations. Therefore, He has promised to get involved, to not allow us to be overwhelmed, and provide that escape. The issue I see with many, and why it seems so overwhelming for us at times is the fact that we are not seeking the escape. We would rather seek to justify and give in to the temptation than seek the escape. Our orders are to seek God in all situations, rely on Him, and take the escape (Proverbs 3:5; 1 Cor. 10:13)!

In all our encounters here in life we must assess the situation. We must see what we are up against. Once you have done this, you must decide based on your walk with God if you must "Break Contact". If the military knows that there will be times they will have to disengage to regroup, resupply, and/or get help. The United States Military, one of the most powerful fighting forces on Earth, then we must accept it is a reality of ours as well. You or I cannot keep going through life thinking, "it's all good, He will forgive me". This is an indifferent attitude, and you will fail time and time again with it. The order is clear. Break contact when needed, to protect yourself and those around you. Poor decisions effect not only you, but all those you do life with. It's not weakness to find the escape, its <u>strength</u>! It is pride that will attempt to move you to do things you are not ready to do. Pride comes before the fall (Proverbs 6:18).

Train How you Fight: *Here we will point out practical ways you can practice/train, so we can attempt to make these Spiritual Disciplines muscle memory.*

This Battle Drill may seem easy enough to plan or practice, however, the hard part is doing it. Therefore, we must "Train How you Fight!" If we do this, we will create a muscle type memory in our minds to put it into action when we feel the sense of being overwhelmed with a situation or temptation. You can put a type of protocol into place. If you are going to a place where you already know there could be this type of overwhelming temptation, have someone you trust know to call and check on you. Have that battle buddy call about an hour into the event/engagement to see if you are ok and lend a hand to get you out of there if needed. This is an essential part of the Battle Drill. In the Battle Drill, the soldiers do not get up and move until there is cover fire for them. The cover fire comes from other soldiers on their team/squad (Battle Buddies). You also would move in pairs if possible while the other two to four squad members give you cover fire. Again, it is very smart to have a person or two you can have call/check on you, or that you can call or go to.

Think about everything in life. When you are unable to handle a situation on your own, you call someone. Be it a tow truck, a mechanic, the Police, etc. You do not cause undue hardship on yourself when you know there are qualified people out there willing and able to help... you just have to reach out to them. In your Church, there are willing and able people who are qualified to provide this type of assistance when needed as well. Another way to practice this is to do your research prior. Take time to find out everything that could be there, and what type of event or gathering it is. This is when you can decide to go or not, and to get the Battle Buddy ready. But you may be asking, "what about those unforeseen moments?" Good question. For those unseen situations we must have a strong relationship with Christ. We must know the Word of God and have passages and verses ready and at the forefront of our minds. This is how Christ combated temptation (Matt. 4), and it is what we need to do.

When you have a strong relationship with God, and you are praying daily, reading the Word daily, you will hear His voice daily and clearer. I remember I went to a party about six months after I was clean and sober. I had a healthy practice of reading the Bible and praying each day, as well as praying about almost everything I was doing each day. When I arrived at the party, I did not feel well. Suddenly, I felt like I should not be there.

The longer I stayed there the stronger the feeling became. The passage that came to mind was 1 Cor. 10:13, out of nowhere. Right then I knew Christ was warning me. I had my "Battle Buddy" (Aline my wife), there with me. I went to her and let her know what I was feeling, and she said we need to go. In that moment I did not argue and tell her, "Lets feel it out some more". Why, you may ask? Because I appointed her as my Battle Buddy, and in combat we trust and have each other's back. In combat, panic and arguing in a Kill Zone (area where the enemy is/or contact is imminent), will get someone hurt. It is better to Break Contact and regroup at the rally point (Home, coffee shop, etc.).

Once we made it home, we found out someone showed up with a controlled substance and was asking others to join in. It was the drug I was addicted to in my teen/young adult years. It would have been very difficult for me to say no. God pointed out the way of escape to me because I was in-tune to His voice, because of the time I spend with Him. I was also able to get away because of the plan I had in place to Break Contact when needed. I accepted my limitations and trusted the protocol I set in place with the guidance of the Holy Spirit. Find a Battle Buddy that you can have check on you. One that is strong in the faith, one that will be there when you need them. One that will give you the cover fire you need to Break Contact when the time comes. And grow that relationship with Christ so you can hear His voice amongst the noises of this world!

Questions for thought:

1. Why is it hard for many to Break Contact, to walk away?

   a. Does it have to do with pride? If not, or if so, why?

2. Share a time you needed to Break Contact. Where you able to find the way of escape? Why or why not?

3. After reading the passage 1 Corinthian 10:6-14; what does this tell you about God?

   a. Has this passage made you see God in a different light? If so, why?

   b. What does this passage tell us about Humanities ability to acknowledge our limitations/weaknesses?

4. Take time to think about how you can put this Battle Drill into practice. Take time to pray about the decision and ask God to guide you to the right protocol.

Chapter 5

REACT TO AMBUSH

Wolves in Sheep's Clothing

Military Explanation:

This Battle Drill is to teach a Squad or Team what to do when they walk into a prepared Kill Zone (Ambush). The ambush is usually initiated by the enemy using casualty-producing devices, and/or a high volume of fire. This Battle Drill covers what to do in a "Near Ambush" and a "Far Ambush".

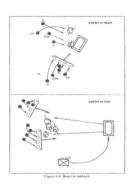

R = Rifleman   GRN = Grenadier
TL = Team Lead   SL = Squad Lead
AR = Automatic Riflemen

Figure 4-6. React to ambush.

In the Near Ambush, the soldiers must immediately return fire and find cover, throw fragmentation grenades or concussion, and smoke grenades. Once they do this, the soldiers must use the opportunity to move out of the Kill Zone/Ambush area. Once they make it though, they must take up positions (cover), to begin an assault on the enemy. It is about the same for the Far Ambush, however, usually you are not in a "Kill Zone", and just have to take covered positions. Once you do this the leader will identify where the enemy is and start the assault on the enemy. If there is any part of your team in the Kill Zone, the part that is not will provide cover fire so those in the near part of the ambush can maneuver to an area they can start the assault.

This Battle Drill has similarities to React to Contact and involves a little of Break Contact as well. The soldiers must start their assault; however, they must also get to a safer area to start the assault. This is why it is important to understand all of the battle drills as you can see, they all overlap in some sort of way. This drill is very intense, and it means the enemy has had time to recon your activity. It means they have had time to see your routine, unit size and strength, and they feel comfortable in attempting to take you out. An ambush takes time and planning, knowing where your enemy is, and preparing to bring the fight to them when ready. Therefore, an ambush is intense and really dangerous if you do not know what to do when it happens (25-101, 2022).

Biblical Parallel:

In the Bible we see many situations where the People of God were ambushed, and we see where they ambushed others in battle (Joshua 8:1-24; Judges 9:31-40; 2 Samuel 3:27; 5:23-25, just to name a few). However, that is not what I want to talk about. I want to discuss the spiritual ambush, the one where others test your resolve. The one where the enemy has been watching you, studying you, waiting for you to become complacent or distracted. There is a Psalm written by King David, Psalm 56, that we will go through. This Psalm will show you that a spiritual ambush is nothing new.

Psalm 56:1-7 (HCSB)

Open Bible for full Chapter

1 Be gracious to me, God, for man tramples me;
he fights and oppresses me all day long.
2 My adversaries trample me all day,
for many arrogantly fight against me.

3 When I am afraid,
I will trust in You.
4 In God, whose word I praise,
in God I trust; I will not fear.
What can man do to me?

5 They twist my words all day long;
all their thoughts against me are evil.

6 They stir up strife, they lurk;
they watch my steps
while they wait to take my life.
7 Will they escape in spite of such sin?
God, bring down the nations in wrath.

In this Psalm, David is describing those that would love to do him harm. They have no remorse, they could not care less about his wellbeing, and they seem proud about their hate toward him ("...arrogantly fight against me." v. 2). It goes on to explain a situation where they are doing all they can to make him fail. They are twisting his words (v.5), they attempt to stir up strife (v.6), and they are watching and waiting to attack (v.6b). This is what the enemy in an ambush is doing. They feel good about their odds to win (arrogant), they set up traps, and other obstacles for the group they want to ambush to get stuck in or have difficulty to move through (stir up strife, twist words, etc.). The goal is your destruction, your downfall (v. 6b; 1 Peter 5:8-9).

The ambush could also be something as easy as another person trying to tempt you to do something you would regret, or you would never usually do. It could be someone with good intentions. We see this type of ambush in Jacobs Mother; she actually ambushes her own sons. In Genesis 27, we see that Isaac was ready to give the blessing and the birth right to Esau his First Born. Esau and Jacobs Mother was listening to this conversation

Isaac was having with Esau (Gen. 27:5). Jacobs Mother went to Jacob, told him what was about to happen, and told him to deceive his father. We know that Jacob does just that, and causes division in his family from listening to this temptation. Jacob was ambushed by his mother that day with news that was too hard to pass up. Jacob was not prepared to handle it and fell.

There are many other stories in the Bible where either the person is being ambushed by someone close with good intentions, or by true enemies. Even Jesus was ambushed, but of course He was ready. In Matthew 22:15-17, is a record of when the Pharisees try to "trap" Jesus with a question. They ambushed Him with a question, hoping He would answer wrong so they could discredit Him or get Him in trouble with the Romans. This is why ambushes are so very dangerous. They come without warning, they come with full force, and they come when you feel comfortable, or weak. We are warned to be ready; we are told to understand the enemy is out there like a lion on the prowl (1 Peter 5:8-9). Ambushes are real, and the enemy likes to use them. The fact is, people like to use them too, and it comes naturally to do something like this to each other due to our sinful nature.

So, what do we do…?

Our Marching Orders:

Our orders are clear and precise. We are told many different times in the Bible to be ready. I have quoted the verse twice now in this chapter, but we are warned that the enemy is like a prowling lion looking to destroy (1 Peter 5:8-9). We are told the enemy is like a thief, stealth, ready to steal and kill (John 10:10). Therefore, we must be ready, we must be aware of our surroundings, and we must know how to react when it happens. The enemies of our life and walk with Christ are always watching. They are waiting for an opportunity to strike, and they have patients. I think the best way to explain the Orders we have to fight an ambush would best be explained, by going through the scenario given in the "Biblical Parallel" portion.

In Psalm 56, we see part of our "Orders" being done by King David. First and foremost, when we want to be prepared for any type of attack, we turn to Jesus. In the Psalm, David talks about his focus on God, his trust in Him. David speaks about praising Him in all of this, not fearing because of who God is. Let me break this down for you. First, in our Orders we are to keep focused on God. Colossians 3:1 tells us to focus on things above, and in Psalms 46 we see that God is our refuge and strength. This means the enemy has less opportunity to ambush us when we are focused on God. Second, we are to trust God (Psalm 56:3). Psalm 46 also tells us that God is ever-present, that He is always there to help and protect us in trouble. God has promised to NEVER leave or forsake us (Matt. 28:20/Hebrews 13:5-6), so we have no reason not to trust God.

Third, we are to praise Him (Psalm 56:4;10). We are to praise God for His Word, for His prevision, for His love. We are to praise Him because we can trust Him, and because of that we will have this assurance that all will be fine. The Psalmist says it best, *"…in God I trust; I will not fear. What can man do to me? (v.11)"* There is nothing really that this world can do to you or I that really matters. We should not fear Man who can only hurt the body, but the one who can destroy body and soul… GOD (Matthew 10:28)! This does not mean you should not take precautions; it means, no matter what happens, you are going to be fine because you have Jesus, and you are in the arms of God! When you have this mentality it creates a life of worship, a life that gives Glory to God minute by minute, hour by hour, day by day, month by month, year by year! And when you do that, the enemy must flee (James 4:7), because you will resist the temptation in the ambush because of the presence you are basking in!

Lastly, we must not retaliate in a sinful way (Psalm 56:7; 11-12). I know in the Military we fight our way out, or we retaliate in a way to hurt the other person, but this is not what God wants. The Psalmist rightly points out, *"… Will they escape in spite of such sin?*

God, bring down the nations in wrath. (v.7)" God will enact His Justice, and He will do it in His time, not ours. He knows what He is doing, and He knows why He waits to punish those that mock Him and deny Him. Our God is a Just and Gracious God, slow to anger and abounding in steadfast love. (Ps. 103:8). Therefore, our orders are to be prepared, trust God, always praise Him, and understand that vengeance is the Lords (Rom. 12:19; Deut. 32:35).

Train How you Fight: *Here we will point out practical ways you can practice/train, so we can attempt to make these Spiritual Disciplines muscle memory.*

> <u>Take a moment:</u> How do we practice this? I will share a few ideas that help me with ambushes, but I want you to take time to think to yourself. Or, if you are with a group, speak amongst each other about some ideas you may have/or things you have done/doing that keep you at the ready for an ambush.

In life I like to say I am living in the "yellow" (cautious). This means I do not live where I fear my own shadow (living in the red). It also does not mean I think nothing bad will every happen (living in the green). The Military and the Word of God taught me this. I understand that we live in a fallen world, a world where bad things happen to good and bad people. Therefore, I attempt to always be focused on God and what He wants. I attempt to always be in communication with Him, so my heart is guarded. When I live in the "yellow", I am aware, and I under-stand that something may come my way that I will have to combat. Someone may flip me off on the road. Someone may steal from me or call me a name. Someone may treat me poorly and speak rudely to me. Someone may know I am a Christian and want me to sin/do something wrong so they can rub it in my face. I know this, so I hold on to Christ daily. I focus on Him, I pray, I am in His Word, I am praising Him in all I do.

When you live with this realization, it comes as no surprise when something happens, when temptation comes, when another tries to "trap" you as they tried to "trap" Jesus. And when it comes as no surprise, the enemy cannot ambush you. They cannot ambush you, because to be ambushed you must be caught off guard, but you can't be caught off guard when you live in the "yellow". On top of that, if we are focused, relying, and trusting in God, and living out our orders (specified in the last section). We would understand that God is all knowing, and if He is all knowing, He saw this coming, and if He saw this coming, He has got it under control. So, rejoice! Of course, we are human though, and the fact is we will at times be caught off guard because we do not perfectly rely on God and turn to Christ in all things. We do not practice what the Psalmist says in Psalm 56 perfectly. A few ways I help myself in situations such as this, is to wear clothing that expresses my faith. When someone flips you off and you realize you are wearing a Jesus shirt, you usually will think twice before retaliating because of the witness it will be. Remember, part of our orders for this Battle Drill is to not retaliate. That is part of what the ambushing party wants out of you. They want you to retaliate so you sin, and when you sin, they have won.

Wearing a Jesus shirt is just one easy way to help you. It is almost like putting a reminder sticky note on yourself to be ready. Another way to help you live in the "yellow" is to always, or at least, most of the time be with fellow believers that want to see you succeed. This way if one of you is "Ambushed" the other can help and keep you on the right track. The last thing you should be ready to do, and practice, is to show love and forgiveness. If we are not to take vengeance into our own hand, then the answer is to show love, forgiveness, and mercy. We are to repay evil with kindness, and we are to love those that persecute us (Matt. 5:43-48). This will grow your faith, glorify God, and cause the person that ambushed you to either not do it again, or seek Christ because of your actions. Ultimately, in all we do, we want to bring more to the saving knowledge of Jesus Christ!

Questions for thought:

1. What were some of the things you have done to not retaliate? Why do you think it worked/why do you think it did not work?

2. Have you ever been Ambushed? Was it someone trying to "Trap" you? Was it someone that had good intensions? What did you do?

3. Why is it hard to not retaliate and wait on the Lord for His Justice?

4. What will you do today to lie in the "Yellow", how do you think this will help you and help bring other to Christ?

Chapter 6

KNOCK OUT BUNKER

The Struggle

Military Explanation:

L et me explain what a Bunker is for those that may not know. A Bunker is an underground, reinforced shelter or defensive position. They can be used for many different things, but in wartime they usually have personnel in them scanning for the enemy. This Battle Drill is conducted when the platoon/team is aware of a bunker, or they receive fire (Contact) from an enemy bunker. The objective of the battle drill is to either destroy the bunker by capturing, killing, or forcing the enemy out of the bunker. The following is what usually happens when a bunker is encountered. First, the platoon/team Reacts to Contact (#2). They would carry out all the steps of this battle drill, which would get them in position to Knock out the Bunker. The platoon lays sufficient suppressive fire on the enemy, they utilize the machine gun in their platoon, to open fire on the Bunker as well. Then a team or squad would find a covered and concealed route and take action to knock out the bunker.

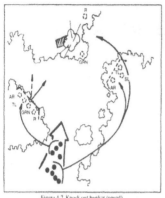

R = Rifleman   GRN = Grenadier
TL = Team Lead   SL = Squad Lead
AR = Automatic Riflemen

Figure 4-7. Knock out bunker (squad).

The goal is to enter the bunker, but first they would usually throw a fragment grenade, or a concussion grenade into the bunker. If anyone would run out, the team providing suppressive fire would take them out, or the team near the bunker would. This battle drill takes coordination, timing, and courage. If the coordination is off, you may shoot a battle buddy. If the timing is off, you may lose the window of opportunity/or give the enemy a chance to recover. If you freeze with fear or do nothing, you will die or get someone else killed. It is important to understand, when you are attacked by a fixed position like a bunker, you will most likely take some casualties. As most bunker positions have heavy weaponry in it. This is the reason it is important to take it out, to knock it out; or it can be tragic for anyone else (allies) that comes by (25-101, 2022).

Biblical Parallel:

For this Battle Drill, I want to focus more on sin that has dug into our lives. Everyone has a sin that they struggle with, a sin that has created a bunker so to speak in their hearts. For some it is lust, or a relationship contrary to what God has ordained, for others it is lying, for some it could be unforgiveness. It will look a little different for everyone, but we all have it. The fact is this sin is there waiting, ready to fight if we want to remove it from our lives, willing to do whatever it takes to stay in our lives. These are the bunkers we must take out. It will take work, it will take coordination, it will take courage. A passage/story in the Bible that I feel illustrates this the best comes from The Gospel of John, in chapter 5.

This story opens explaining the belief about the Pool of Bethesda. It was believed that an *"…angel would go down into the pool from time to time and stir up the water. Then the first one who got in after the water was stirred up recovered from whatever ailment he had (v. 4)"*. So, you could imagine, this place was filled with the sick, the lame, the hurt, and the suffering of the land. Everyone there was seeking hope, desperate for it, and would do wherever they had to for it. The story goes on telling us of a man that was there, and scripture tells us that he was there for a long time. It also tells us that he had been sick/lame for 38 years. This was a man seeking hope, but at the same time it would seem he had lost it. Then Jesus enters the scene in verse 6; the source of hope, the source of freedom, the promise walking in. We are told that He (Jesus) knows this man had been there for a while. Jesus was on a mission, and we see that Jesus walked right up to him. It was not a random meeting, Jesus wanted to "Knock out a Bunker"!

Jesus asks the man if he wants to get well, and if he wants to be healed? The man answers with a complaint. Scripture says, *"Sir,"* *the sick man answered, "I don't have a man to put me into the pool when the water is stirred up, but while I'm coming, someone goes down ahead of me. (v.7)"""* He pretty much admits that there is a "dug in position" in his life that he cannot get past, one he cannot defeat. Every time he attempts to, he is defeated. This situation he is in, is the bunker. We do not know what happened to him, how he got there, if it was an accidental injury, or if someone hurt him. We know he was not born that way, as scripture stated a time period for the ailment. Since then, it would seem he was trying everything to overcome and take out this bunker in his life. The "Bunker" (his sickness/injury) drove away his family, friends, and now it was taking/destroying his hope. He sat there, but he did not think he would ever overcome his situation, *"…but while I'm coming, someone goes down ahead of me. (v.7b)"*

At that moment though, Jesus told him to get up, to pick up his mat and walk. The man did just that, he got up and walked away with his mat. This bunker in his life was destroyed by Jesus Christ in an instant. Did he look baffled? Did he get up slowly? Did he have a second of doubt? We are not told, but what we see from the story is the man IMMEDIATELY responding at the word of Jesus, and at that moment the bunker in his life was destroyed. Was his life perfect after that, was it without hardship, no. We know this because he was confronted by the Religious Leaders right after, and they were harassing him about carrying a mat. His life was not perfect after this, but he was free. The bunker that caused so much loss was gone, and now he was able to truly experience peace and the fruit of Hope in Jesus.

I hope you get what I am trying to convey here. We have stuff in our lives, things that have caused heart ache, pain, and loss. It was brought on by our sin, or by another's (someone else wronging us). This hurt, this pain, this sin has "dug in", and it does not want to leave. It is the sin that we struggle with day in and day out. This sin we do not want to do, but when we try not to do it, we do it anyways. Does this sound familiar? Paul says it best when he says, *"15 For I do not understand what I am doing, because I do not practice what I want to do, but I do what I hate. 16 And if I do what I do not want to do, I agree with the law that it is good. 17 So now I am no longer the one doing it, but it is sin living in me. 18 For I know that nothing good lives in me, that is, in my flesh.*

For the desire to do what is good is with me, but there is no ability to do it. 19 For I do not do the good that I want to do, but I practice the evil that I do not want to do. 20 Now if I do what I do not want, I am no longer the one doing it, but it is the sin that lives in me." (Rom. 7:15-20)

Paul had a Bunker in his life too. It is a daily struggle he is pointing out, and he is saying it always takes casualties. He is always running into it, and it is always a battle. Whatever Paul is struggling with has dug in, and he tells us later the only person that can help with this battle is the Lord (Jesus). There is no avoiding it, and no "living with it", the bunker must go! In Romans 7:24-25 Paul says, *"What a wretched man I am! Who will rescue me from this dying body? 25 I thank God through Jesus Christ our Lord!"* Who will save you, who will rescue you, who will knock out that bunker with you as your team leader? Jesus Christ! Without Him we are slaves to our sinful nature that always submits to the bunkers in our lives.

With me, the bunker was addiction. No matter what I did, I kept falling back into it. I could not take it out, and it was taking everything from me, just like the injury/disease the man sitting at the Pool of Bethesda. For 29 years I was at war with this bunker, and I had to come to terms that there was no way around it… it had to be knocked out for me to be better. That was only possible because of God through Jesus Christ our Lord! "Thank you Jesus for coming to me when I was at my lowest, sitting by my pool of Bethesda!"

Our Marching Orders:

Our orders here are very simple, yet hard for many to do. It involves dying to oneself, to pick up your cross daily and humbly follow Christ. The Bible says in Matt. 16:24-26, *"Then Jesus said to His disciples, "If anyone wants to come after Me, let him deny himself, and take up his cross, and be following Me. For whoever wants to save his life will lose it. But whoever loses his life for My sake will find it. For what will a person be profited if he gains the whole world, but forfeits his life? Or what will a person give in-exchange-for his life?"* This illustrates our death. To pick up one's cross is to accept Capital Punishment, and Christ is saying we must do this to have life. 2 Cor. 5:17 says that our old self has "passed away". Christ took the punishment, but we still have a decision to make every day. This all points out, that the only way to get through a bunker is to submit to the Will of God, to let Christ lead, to have Him as Lord and Savior. It does not end there however, because these verses show that it is a daily decision. We will battle with ourselves daily to do the opposite of what we should do (Rom. 7:15-20).

It is in our tendency to attempt to take the bunker on our own, or in our own way. Then, when we are unable to, we make excuses that prolong the issue and hurt us and those around us. We need to turn to Christ and accept His command as Commander and Chief in our lives to overcome the bunkers, as did the sick man at the Pool of Bethesda (he allowed Christ to lead). I think this is hard for many because of our "individualistic" type culture. We do not like to ask for help, many do not want a handout, or feel like they need "charity". This mentality goes against the way God expects us to treat each other. We are to look out for "others" (Phil 2:1-4) and seek their prosperity. We are to morn, rebuke, lift-up and correct each other in all we do (2 Tim. 3:16; Rom. 15:2). So, when God expects us to do it with each other, He definitely expects this type of partnership when it comes to doing life with Him as our Lord (John 15:5-7).

To drive the point home on our orders, I want you to ask yourself why it is so hard to allow God to lead you? Why do we always what to be in control, when our plans seem to fail every time. I feel it leads back to the original sin. You see, even Adam and Eve decided at one point to "take" it for themselves (Knowledge of Good and evil). They felt they knew best, and they could do it on their own (Gen. 3 the fall). God created us in a way where we would do life with Him. We were to learn from Him and cultivate a relationship with Him as we "prospered and cultivated the land" (Gen 1:27-28). Once we (Humans) took the key ingredient if you will, out of the equation (the "ingredient" being God Almighty). We through a monkey wrench into the system called creation. We can do nothing without God. Yet even though we do this daily (attempt to do it without Him), God shows us grace and is there waiting for us to allow Him back in (2 Peter 3:9).

The part of the issue that makes it hard to turn back to God and allow Him to lead is our pride. Think about it. No one wants to admit they failed, no one wants to feel useless or like they have let someone down. These feelings lead us down a path of self-preserving pride. We are trying to protect our ego instead of humbly submitted to God when He is right there, lovingly waiting for us to call out to Him. The Bible is very clear that pride is dangerous. We are told that this Pride is what will occur before we fall (sin, fail, etc.) (Prov. 16:18). God opposes the proud and favors the humble (James 4:6). Why? Because this Pride keeps you from God, being humble draws you toward Him. Why should you let go of pride? Because God promises to lift you up when you humble yourself (James 4:10).

Our Marching Orders are clear. We are to trust God with all we do, we are to turn to Him in our time of need. We must let go of pride and selfish ambition, and do life with God, with Him as our leader, and move when He says move. This is the only way we will "Knock out a Bunker".

Train How you Fight: *Here we will point out practical ways you can practice/train, so we can attempt to make these Spiritual Disciplines muscle memory.*

There could be many techniques in creating muscle memory in our lives when it comes to knocking out a bunker. It really involves submitting to the Will of God, and allowing Him to lead, trusting that He knows best. You may be saying, "that is easier said than done", and you are right. I have realized that in instances where it seems like an impossible task to remember to do something, use an Acronym. Yes, that is right, an Acronym. The Military loves to use them, and they make them up for all occasions. The fact remains, that Acronyms are amazing at helping us remember things we want to recall quickly and systematically. The acronym that helps me with this spiritual discipline is S.O.A.P. This acronym comes from The Salvation Army Church and is used when teaching the Youth how to read Scripture and apply it to their lives. It teaches them to apply it in a very purposeful and meaningful way, that helps keep what they have read in context. To practice this technique, you do not need a degree, you do not need to be a teacher, or a scholar. It is simple and very easy to use all the time individually, or in small or large groups. The amazing thing about this tool is, it helps you put God and His word first in all that you do when you apply it to more than just your daily Bible reading.

<u>S.O.A.P</u>

<u>S</u>criptures:

It's all about the Word of God! Right when a Bunker pops up and attacks, or a situation occurs when you should put God first (God should be part of everything). The first thing you need to do is stop and consult the Word of God. Scripture is what we are to measure everything up to. Scripture tells us what we should do, what we should not do, and it also gives us ways to apply these truths. It reveals who God is and what He wants. How does it do all this, well, the scriptures of the Old and New Testament were given by inspiration by God, and they alone constitute the Divine rule of our daily Christian faith and practices. There are a few ways our modern Bibles do this. Some Bibles have a topical index, a section that helps you find verses that speak on certain life issues and situations. For example, it would have the word "anxiety" and then list all the verses in the Bible that speak on it. You can also use a Biblical dictionary or concordance to find these key words to look up in scripture.

I like to open the Bible and allow the Holy Spirit to lead. I try to read the Bible every day, so I am good at going to a book of the Bible that I know has some stories or situations similar to what I am going through. Then I read! I usually do not just read the section once, I will read it a few times, and sometimes I read it again in a different translation (one time in NIV, and the other is ESV). This helps me pull the meaning out (exegesis) if I am a little confused with some of the wording. Once this is complete, you would take it to the next step in the acronym.

Observation:

This is the part where you really dive into prayer. You should be doing this whole technique with an attitude of prayer, but this part is where you must literally bring it before God in deep prayer. Asking Him, "Why did you write this?", or "help me see what you want me to learn…". You can also, as I have already stated, read the scripture you are praying about in other translations to see if that will bring more clarity. You can also consult Commentaries. Commentaries are books that panels of Bible Scholars put together about books of the Bible that break down dates, times, locations, context, cultural context, etc. This can help with your observation and cultivate proper exegesis. So, you pray, and pray, and ask, and wait, waiting for God to guide you and speak into your life. This could be the hardest part. You could say this because, we (Humans) do not have very good patients. We want the answers now, and we do not want to feel uncomfortable for any amount of time.

Application

This is where you take what you know, or feel you know that God wants you to do, and you plan. You are still in a prayerful mindset, and you ask God what He would like you to do with the truth He has just revealed to you. You can write it down or not, just formulate how you will put this truth into practice. How can you take this head knowledge and get it to your heart, to become part of you when you act?

Prayer

This is where you strictly pray. You thank God for what He revealed, for being there for you. Then you pray that He will continue to guide you as you execute what was decided on in the "Application" part of the technique. You ask Him to stop you if you are about to act based off your own emotion or intension, as you want Him to lead.

This whole process seems like a lot of work, and it seems like it would take a very long time. The truth is, it will take as long as you put into it. There will be times where this process goes as fast as 5 minutes. Why? Because you must make a quick decision. The fact is, the more you do this the faster you will be able to do it. This process could take 30 mins to 3 hours or more. It all depends on the situation, the time you have to act, and the motivation you have to do it. Is it worth taking a little longer to ensure you consult God? Is it worth making the other party or person wait to ensure you are honoring God in all that you do? Is it worth swallowing your pride and admitting you need His help to Knock out the Bunker? These are some questions you must ask yourself if you think this technique is a waste of time. Maybe you found a better way to practice this, good. Do it then!

The fact remains that we must train how we fight, and the Bible is clear that the only way to Knock out those Bunkers/issues in your life that have "dug in" (bitterness; hatred; malice; addiction; unforgiveness, etc.), is to allow Christ to work in and though you as He did with the Man at the Pool of Bethesda. We cannot do it on our own strength, and when you practice this acronym in all hard decisions. It will become muscle memory when you run into a bunker. Don't let pride lead, it will only lead to destruction!

Questions for thought:

1. Why do we always want to handle these Bunkers in our lives on our own?

    a. What makes you think twice to seek help or to seek God?

2. Why do many people attempt to live with, or ignore the Bunkers in their lives?

    a. What are some things you will do today to break this unhealthy habit?

3. Share some other ideas on how you can "Train how you fight" when it comes to Knocking out the Bunkers in life?

4. Are you an Optimist or a Pessimist? How does this effect your decision making when in situations like this? What can you do to sustain or change this outlook?

Chapter 7

ENTER
BUILDING AND CLEAR

Sanctification/Holiness

Military Explanation:

For Military training, I would have to admit that this is my favorite Battle Drill to practice. It involves each person to pay attention to the group, to move as a unit, and to flow like a smooth stream. The goal of this drill is to kill, forces a withdrawal, or capture all of the enemy in the building. The team must ensure to prevent any noncombatant casualties and collateral damage in accordance with the "Rules of Engagement" (ROE). The other goal the team wants to meet is, to ensure they have a sufficient fighting force to defeat anything the enemy would throw at them as well as to be able to continue the mission. I will explain how this drill works in a little more detail.

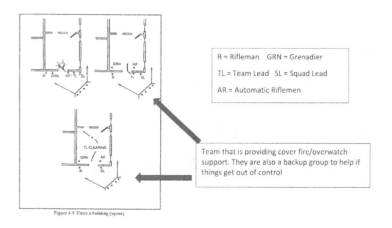

Figure 4-9. Enter a building (squad)

Once the platoon has cover fire, and they have determined their flank and have marked it for other units to be aware. The platoon will pick a squad to enter the building, and the leader of the squad will determine the way in which he wants them to enter (there are a few methods to choose from). Above you will see a diagram from the Military Manuel showing these choices.

As you can see there are a few ways the squad/team can "Stack" on the wall to enter the building. The team is to enter and secure a foot hold of the building. They teach a specific way to enter so you are not rushing, and you do not bump into another soldier causing a bottleneck at the door (this could lead to the death of those soldiers). The saying they teach is "slow is smooth, and smooth is fast". By the time the first person enters and the enemy targets them, the second team member is entering taking out this enemy soldier if the first one did not see them, and this is how it goes until the whole team/squad is in the room. Then, after you take a room, you mark it in a way to tell others in the unit that this room has been cleared. The platoon will usually utilize the first room as a rally point for others to come to, and/or bring wounded to (to keep the initial foot hold). Once the whole building is cleared, the platoon moves to the next building (25-101, 2022).

Biblical Parallel:

In the Bible we know that when we accept Christ, we are a New Creation (2 Cor. 5:17). We also know that we are instantly saved/washed clean by the Blood of Christ (Mark 16:16; Rom. 10:9; 1 John 5:4; John 3:16-17). However, there is a lifelong journey you enter into when you are saved. This is "Sanctification", and it affects us two ways. The first is instant as I have mentioned above, which is where we are forgiven and become New Creations. The second is what Believer's call "Your Walk" with Christ. Your "Walk" is a lifelong journey, it is where you grow, mature, and cultivate a deep relationship with God through His Son Jesus Christ. The Biblical Parallel for this has to do with allowing God to clear out all those bad habits, habits that are considered ungodly and sinful. I see it as clearing a "room" in your head, which counts as the "building". Each time you allow Christ into a "room" in your head, Christ will clear out all the sin, and anything you do not need/that is holding you back in your "Walk".

I believe Paul puts it the best when he tells the Church in Philippi this.

> *15 Therefore, all who are mature should think this way. And if you think differently about anything, God will reveal this also to you. 16 In any case, we should live up to whatever truth we have attained. 17 Join in imitating me, brothers, and observe those who live according to the example you have in us. (Philippians 3:15-17).*

I feel this was put beautifully by Paul by inspiration of the Holy Spirit. This is what we also should remember when walking alongside new believers as they grow.

Let me explain what Paul is getting at here. In this Book (Philippians), Paul is telling the Church in Philippi how they should be living to share and represent the Gospel of Christ (Ch. 1). Paul explains in some detail how they should be acting toward each other and their community as followers of Christ. How they should treat each other (Ch. 2), Christ's example for us (Ch. 2), our goal and what unites us (Ch. 3), etc. Then he points out something very important for us to understand. The fact is, not all Christians, especially new to the faith Christians, will always agree with what we are sharing with them. For example, you may tell them that cursing is not ok, and they should attempt to stop using words like that. They may think to themselves that it is not a big deal. Paul is telling us, that this is ok. Why? Because all we must do is encourage them to continue their "walk" with Christ, and He (Christ) will eventually give them the revelation. Prompting them to change their language to something that represents Christ correctly. We have already told them what scripture says, now it is up to God and their free will. We are to continue being an example to them, *"Join in imitating me, brothers, and observe those who live according to the example you have in us" (v.17).* Not only being an example, however, but still being there to correct, rebuke, encourage, and morn with them. This will allow the Holy Spirit to "Clear the Room" so to speak in their head and further their Sanctification (Christlikeness).

We have lived a life of sin, and now we have Christ, the means to combat this sinful nature of ours. The only way to get rid of all the bad habits is to search your heart and allow God to clear it of all unrighteousness. As the Psalmist says in Psalm 139:23-24, *"Search me, God, and know my heart; test me and know my anxious thoughts. See if there is any offensive way in me, and lead me in the way everlasting".* Pretend your mind is a building. Your mind is full of things you have experienced, done, said, and things that have been done to you. These things and events are good and bad. They have created habits, and they helped define your character/who you are today. Your head has many rooms that you store all this stuff in, and unless you open the door and let God in, you will never clear it. Once you are saved, you then start your journey with Christ, allowing Him into each room one at a time. With His leadership and guidance, you allow Him to clear each one. This means you will face things from your past you may not want to, and you may have to relive things you thought you were over. But there is no way to truly put to death your old self unless you do this.

Therefore, as explained earlier in this book, you will need a Battle Buddy (someone to disciple you/mentor you). By doing this you will be able to work through these rooms Christ is clearing with you. When you are "Clearing" rooms with Christ, keep in mind the saying I mentioned earlier; "slow is smooth, smooth is fast". It is very important because if you get ahead of the leader (Christ), things will not go well. When you move as a unit, the enemy does not have time to hurt you or react. They will focus on the first to enter, then when they notice another coming in, they are distracted, giving enough time for the first or second person to take them out. We must move this way with God. We are to listen to His guidance, instruction, and allow Him to lead us into the room. When you go in alone, or you go in relying on your own power, it will be bad. If you step in front of God when clearing these "Rooms" in your head, it could cause you to sin or hurt those you love around you. For example, say you are entering a "room" that houses your addiction part of your old self. And you do it on your own strength and leave Christ out of it. You will most likely fall back into addiction/relapse because, only Christ can overpower the sin in our lives.

To sum this all up. The Biblical parallel is our sinful habits and tendencies we need to get rid of. The only way to get rid of them is to deal with them one by one (as you clear each room, one by one), with the leadership, guidance, and power of Christ. Only through submitting to His Will, and allowing the Holy Spirit to prompt you when it is time to enter, will you be able to "Enter and Clear the Building" of your life to continue your lifelong journey of sanctification. It is the only way to move closer toward a life that is Christ-like, one that honors God, furthers His Kingdom, and brings more to the saving knowledge of Jesus Christ through your example.

Our Marching Orders:

What are we to do? Psalms 139 is a great section of Scripture to use as our "Marching Orders" in this battle drill. Right from the start in verse one the psalmist points out his realization of who God is and what He is capable of. *"Lord, You have searched me and known me. You know when I sit down and when I stand up; You understand my thoughts from far away." (Ps. 139:1-2)* God is the all-knowing one, and only He knows everything about you, so it would be smart to have Him (Christ), lead. So, first, our orders are to let Him lead! Then the psalmist goes on to share the fact that God is everywhere, always, and in everything. There is not a place in our existence you cannot find God. *"Where can I go to escape Your Spirit? Where can I flee from Your presence? If I go up to heaven, You are there; if I make my bed in Sheol, You are there. If I live at the eastern horizon or settle at the western limits; even there Your hand will lead me; (Ps. 139:7-10).*

The second part of our orders when it comes to this battle drill is, to understand this is a team effort. God is your battle buddy here, and He will never leave nor forsake you. The only danger that can happen is you walk away from Him, or step in front of Him. This realization goes with the first part of the Order. Let Him lead! You can pretend all you want, and attempt to do this on your own, but the fact remains that it is not possible without Him (God). It is something only He can do, and you must submit and follow. The third part of this order involves submitting to His Will. Submitting in such a way that you will follow, no matter the uncertainty of what you think, or do not think He will find or ask of you. In the last part of the Psalm, David, the psalmist asks God to do something that makes him (David) vulnerable. He asks God to take a deep dive into his thoughts, mind, heart/his very being to see if there is anything that is not worthy to be in the presence of our King!

> *Psalms 139:23-24 (HCSB)*
> *"23 Search me, God, and know my heart;*
> *test me and know my concerns.*
> *24 See if there is any offensive way in me;*

lead me in the everlasting way."

This is key to our orders, and is key to the success of the mission at hand when it comes to clearing the "Building" of your soul/mind/being. David is asking God to search him. This is not a "search" me like in a casual sense. It is not comparable to the type of search you would do around the house if you were looking for a snack (slightly peckish). Oh no! The Hebrew word here is (h**āqar**) **pronounced, "khaw-kar'"**. It is translated in the Bible six different ways. They are; search, search out, found out, seek out, seek, sounded, and try. The definition of this word found in the Strong's Dictionary states, "khaw-kar', a primitive root; properly, to penetrate; hence, to examine intimately; - find out, (Make) search (out), seek... Did you catch it? "...*to penetrate/to examine intimately!* He is saying, "God, I am ready for you to search every inch of me, nothing is off limits for you". If we do not come before God with this type of humility and sub-mission, our mission will fail.

In verse 24, David takes it a step further. He not only asks God to search him in a way that leaves nothing untouched, but he adds the request for God to lead him in the everlasting way. David is asking God to remove anything unrighteous, worldly, or sinful that is found. The phrase "Everlasting Way" found at the end of the Psalm literally means, "way of eternity". God's way, the way that can be attributed to the very attributes/nature of

God (Hibbard and Whedon, 1909). We are to want God to take the lead, we are to stay with Him, and submit to Him fully. Then once this is done, allow Him to work in our lives to make us more like Christ, to clear the room of our heart that is so full of unrighteousness. Please keep in mind that this will not be easy. There will be things found that we may still enjoy. There may be things found we do not want to deal with because of the memories it recalls. There could be things we want to avoid because it will involve us going and reconciling with another, (which can be very uncomfortable).

Whatever it may be, or whatever He (God) may find. Our orders are to submit to the Will of God and His guidance willingly, humbly, and whole heartedly. There is no room for the solo commando. There is no room for pride, or conceit. When clearing buildings in Afghanistan or in Iraq. If anyone on the team stepped out of line, thought they could do it alone, or wanted to show off, someone was hurt. Either themselves or one of their battle buddies. It is the same here, we must stick to the plan, and stick to our training, or the enemy will keep their foot hold.

Train How you Fight: *Here we will point out practical ways you can practice/train, so we can attempt to make these Spiritual Disciplines muscle memory.*

Go to scripture and put yourself in their shoes. What do I mean by that? It is where you put yourself in the situation of the story, or event you are reading about in the Bible. This practice is something that will take time to master, because it is easy to talk yourself out of it and give an excuse not to do it that day or time you are reading the Bible. This practice heavily relies on your battle buddies in your life. You can relate it to a New Year's Resolution for example. Many people say they will go to the gym and start to be healthier, but if they do not have anyone holding them accountable, it is easy for the person to make excuses not to go, or not to eat well that day. "I have a lot to do today." Or "ill go tomorrow." "I forgot to pack a lunch; Ill go buy fast food just today." Then this happens again the next day, and the next, until you do not do the resolution anymore.

So, the first thing to set up for this training, is to inform your Battle Buddy, your support group, those that mentor/disciple you and hold you accountable. These brothers and sisters in Christ need to be informed and onboard to help you, or it will not work/or it will not work for long. Once that is complete, then you need to set up how often you would like there help. Do you want them to check in on you once a week, once every other week, every other day, etc. After you get your support group, and you have a plan on how to carry it out, an easy way you can approach this training involves an acronym. You know me, I love my acronyms… the Military has just imbedded this type of remembering into how I do things. Let's check this one out.

L.E.A.D

L: Listen to what God is saying to you in the study you are doing, or in the passage you are reading. Share it with your group. Discuss this with your group and battle buddies and get their thoughts and experiences from how God spoke to them regarding this lesson/truth/rebuke, etc. Then you need to pray about what you leaned and studied and be open to God's message. Do not try to explain it away because it is a hard truth, or because you disagree. We do not know best, God does, and He has created, allowed, and done what He has done for a reason.

E: Employ the teaching you have just learned into your everyday life rationally. Apply it to work (how are you treating people at work?). If the truth you have learned is about forgiving or being patient, how are you living this truth out? Do you hold grudges? Are you unforgiving to certain people in your life? Do you get irritated with others easily, etc.? Take it to pray with God, and ask the questions David did in his Psalm, *"23 Search me, God, and know my heart; test me and know my concerns. 24 See if there is any offensive way in me; lead me in the everlasting way. (Ps. 139:23-24)"*. This is the part where you identify with God the room in your heart/head that you will be clearing (with the guidance of the Holy Spirit). These issues or habits could have been formed because of life experiences, taught by parent examples, etc. You formulate a plan of how to put this truth into practice. You should create a plan with the guidance of God and the knowledge from your mentor/group.

A: Adhere to the plan and the teaching of God's word. You need to stay focused on putting His Word into practice, and to use the knowledge of those that are mentoring you and discipling you. Keep going to God in prayer, keep asking for His guidance, strength, and endurance in this process. Why? Because it will take time, and it will be hard, and you will want to talk yourself out of it. This is also the part where you can ask yourself, "how can I stay true to the truth I have learned?" What do you need to stop, what do you need to avoid? What do you have to add to your everyday routine, etc.?

D: Decide to live according to God's will. It is not enough to plan, and seek His Will, if you do not make a deliberate and conscious decision to live it out. This would involve a desire to improve your life by deciding to change it however you must, to humbly submit to the Will of God. Which will help you grow for the better even if it's hard or you do not feel like it. Living it out will help you to become more Christ-like, so your past experiences from mistakes and sin can become your testimony of what you have overcome in Christ Jesus!

As you can see, to train how you fight here involves a lot. Just as it would in a war zone when clearing a building. There is training, insight from leaders, guidance from leaders, coordination, and implementation of strategies. You must follow orders, and trust your battle buddies, as well as your leaders. If you do not, or you attempt to do it alone, there will be casualties. You may be asking why the acronym is LEAD. It is LEAD because, if you are doing this, you are a leader. You are going to be the example for those that are "younger" in the faith, that will see your example and learn from how you do things. This is what discipleship is, it is doing life with others, learning from others, and growing together in Christ. Paul also encourages this type of example.

> *1 Corinthians 4:16-17*, "*16 Therefore I urge you to imitate me. 17 This is why I have sent Timothy to you. He is my dearly loved and faithful son in the Lord. He will remind you about my ways in Christ Jesus, just as I teach everywhere in every church.*

> *1 Corinthians 11:1*, "*Imitate me, as I also imitate Christ.*"

Paul is urging the Church in Corinth to follow his example as he grows, and lives out everything God, in Christ has taught and shown him. The discipline described in this chapter is important for you to grow, but it is also really important for others to grow around you. There will come a point where you will not just be a "Timothy" (one being discipled), but a "Paul" (the one doing the Discipling). You will always be a Disciple because you will never know it all. However, you will one day also be the mentor doing it for another as well. So, allow God into your heart, ask Him to search it and clean it. Work with the Holy Spirit to rid yourself of those worldly habits and tendencies so you will grow in faith and righteousness.

Questions for thought:

1. Why do we want to lock the door to certain parts of our life and throw away the key?

   a. It is usually easier for us to help someone else with issues in their life then ask for help with ours.

2. If you are willing to, share one of these issues in life that is hard for you to "Clear".

   a. Why is it hard?

   b. Why have you not trusted the Lord to take care of it?

3. Do you have any other ideas to implement this "Battle Drill"? If so, what is it?

4. Why do we think we can ignore an issue, and pretend it will go away or disappear?

   a. It is fear that you do not want to become that, (whatever it is) again?

Chapter 8

ENTER A
TRENCH AND CLEAR

Entrenched Sin

Military Explanation:

T he purpose of this Drill is to train the platoon or squad to secure a foothold in a trench. The squad is to kill, capture, or force the withdrawal of the enemy, ensuring you also defeat their counterattack if there is any. Then, continue the mission as planned. First, they would react to contact (Battle Drill #2). The team that is in direct contact with the enemy locates their position and suppresses them. The leader will then determine if they can maneuver by identifying the following.

- The actual trench, and any obstacles.

- The size of the enemy forces, as well as their weaponry (automatic weapons, vehicles, etc.).

- A point of entry (with a covered and concealed route to the entry point).

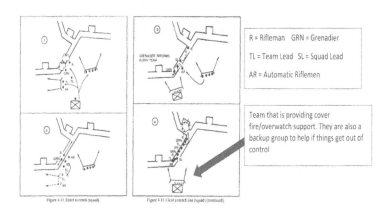

R = Rifleman   GRN = Grenadier

TL = Team Lead   SL = Squad Lead

AR = Automatic Riflemen

Team that is providing cover fire/overwatch support. They are also a backup group to help if things get out of control

Figure 4-11. Enter a trench (squad).

Figure 4-11. Clear a trench line (squad) (continued).

Once this is determined, the team that is not in direct fire will conduct the maneuver to enter and start the initial clearing. This team will, upon entering the trench, destroy or suppress the enemy and their weapons, and continue to give close suppressive fire on the enemy in the trench throughout the contact. Once there is a foothold, the leader of this team will signal more of the team/squad/platoon to enter the trench at their location. They will also direct the suppressing team giving cover fire to shift fire, to get any fleeing enemy soldiers. The leader will illuminate the entry point for the rest of the team/squad/

platoon. While in the trench the team will start to move through and clear each path, and/or room in the trench. If needed they will use grenades and concussion grenades. Once cleared, they will radio this in, check supplies, personnel, and ammunition. If there is a need for a resupply, they will report this as required (25-101, 2022).

Biblical Parallel:

This Battle Drill is related to the last one, "Enter and Clearing a Building". A "Trench" is an event, situation, or action you were part of, committed, or it happened to you that you won't let go of. It's worse than the rooms, as it is dug in, has many enemies guarding it, and they have heavy weapons and vehicles so to speak. It is the part of your past or present you want to ignore, something you wish would disappear, but it won't unless you address it. A good Biblical example of this comes from the book of Isaiah. In chapter 6, Isaiah is in the presence of God, in the Divine Throne room. There he sees Seraphim (angels), the Divine seated and the Seraphim worshiping God Almighty. The worship was so intense the foundations of the doorways shook at the sound of their voices, and the temple was filled with smoke (Isaiah 6:4).

Then Isaiah said, *"Woe is me for I am ruined because I am a man of unclean lips and live among a people of unclean lips, and because my eyes have seen the King of Lord of Hosts"* (Isaiah 6:5). At this point one of the Seraphim flew to him and with a glowing coal that was from the altar, touched Isaiah's mouth with it and said that his wickedness was removed, and sins atoned for (6:6). You may be wounding how this relates to what I shared above, so I will explain. Isaiah knew his people were full of sin. They did not regard the commands of the Lord; they lived a life that conformed to the nations around them. They worshiped other gods and there was even child sacrifice being conducted and carried out for these other gods. To say the least, there were things that Isaiah felt were unforgivable that were happening. Acts of evil that were ignored by the religious leaders, and people of God in general.

So, when he was in the presence of a Holy and Just God, he knew he was done for. You cannot be in the presence of a Holy and righteous God without consequences. But instead of judgement and condemnation, there was forgiveness, grace, and mercy. God took care of the situation and made it possible for Isaiah to not only serve Him but stand Holy and right before Him. What we see here is, no matter what you have done, no matter your past, or even the present. If you will humbly submit to God, He can make it all right. He is willing and faithful to forgive (1 John 1:9). He is the one that will go into the "trench" and clear it. You do not have to avoid God because you are too ashamed of what you did, or how you live. God has already taken care of it on the Cross (Isaiah 53:11; Hebrews 9). When Christ died, He did so to conquer all sin, death, and He did if for all people, for all time. All we must do is humbly accept Christ as Lord and give our hearts to God, and we will be cleansed.

Another biblical story that gives a picture to the other side of this dilemma of entrenched sin can be found in Joshua 6 starting at verse 15 through 19, and chapter 7. The other story with Isaiah displayed what God would do with a humble, repentant, and willing heart. Here we will see what happens when we continue to avoid it, hide it, or justify it. In this passage God instructed Joshua and the Israelites to destroy everything in the fortified city of Jericho except for Rahab and her family. They were also instructed that all silver, gold, and articles of bronze and iron were dedicated to the Lord (6:15-19). Since they were set apart for the Lord, anyone that took from these things would be guilty of sin. Then in chapter 7 of Joshua we find out that one man, Achan, was unfaithful. This sin was held against all the community, as verse one says, *"The Israelites, however, were unfaithful regarding the things set apart for destruction. Achan son of Carmi, son of Zabdi, son of Zerah, of the tribe of Judah, took some of what was set apart... (7:1)"* Before anyone found out, Joshua sends a few thousand Men to attack and take a place called Ai. Now this should have been an easy battle, an easy win, especially when compared to the victory they just had through God, in Jericho. However, because of Achan's disobedience they lost.

The rest of the story in Chapter 7 explains how Joshua mourned and pleaded with God because of the defeat and inquired why there was a defeat. (7:6-9). Then God reveals to him what happened, and why they lost. God informs Joshua that there will be no victory, no blessing, until this sin is taken care of. So, Joshua and the rest of the Leaders of Israel find out it was Achan, and they carry out the punishment for the sins. This story is a great example of what not to do when confronting the Trench in your life. It shows the danger, and just how much destruction it can cause. Achan knew he was not allowed to take the things he did, and he kept this sin hidden. He did not want anyone to find out, he tried to continue life as if nothing ever happened. So, this sin became a trench in his life. This trench/sin affected everyone around him, as does all sin. It stopped and hindered his walk with God, and it physically hurt people around him (36 men died in the attack of Ai because of this disobedience). When there is hidden sin in our life, it will hurt those around you. It does not matter if you pretend it is not there, it will come to light (Eccl. 12:14). It will continue to hinder your walk, and harm your family, friends; pretty much all the relationships around you until you address it.

Now, in this story with Achan, he never came forward and repented. He had to be confronted by the Lord essentially through Joshua. They literally had to go tribe by tribe, clan, by clan, family by family, until they got to Achan. He might have been hoping he would get lucky, and he would not be found out. Maybe he thought someone else would take the fall or did something even worse so he would be overlooked. We just don't really know why he did not come forward right away, but, after he was caught and confessed, he was put to death for his sin. This is still a possibility for any follower of God if we never address the sin that has become a "Trench" in our lives. Not necessarily physical death, but spiritual death. Therefore, it is so important to address it now with the guidance and help of the Holy Spirit. We cannot be ashamed of a particular sin in our lives to the point we try to ignore it, or hold on to it, and bring about undue hardship on ourselves because of it. We must give it to God and put it at the foot of the Cross!

The sin in our lives that becomes entrenched is deadly and can only be overcome by Christ. When we ignore it, it creates destruction. When we hide it, it harms those around us. When we attempt to justify it, we bring condemnation on ourselves. But with Christ, and the guidance of the Holy Spirit, these trenches will be entered and cleared because of the gift and sacrifice of Christ Jesus. With both stories discussed in this chapter, we see two different ways to handle the trenches in our lives. We also see that entrenched sin exists and how this battle drill is very relevant for us. But now that we see what it means biblically regarding Trenches... what are our marching orders?

Our Marching Orders:

I think the best way to address the "Marching Orders for Entering and Clearing a Trench" is best illustrated by the example of King David when comforted with the entrenched sin in his life. This story can be found in 2 Samuel 11 - 12 (Please take the time to read these chapters). Let me paint the picture of what happened really quick. David had just committed adultery with one of his soldiers' wives. He saw her bathing and sent for her. He had sexual relations with her, and she became pregnant. David wanted to cover up this sin. So, he sent for her husband Uriah and brought him back from battle so he could spend time with his wife, hoping he would sleep with her. David did this so the child would be assumed to be Uriah's. This plan did not work, therefore David had Uriah sent to the front lines, and pretty much put him in a situation where he would defiantly die. This order was carried out, and Uriah died in combat. Therefore, David murdered Uriah in the hopes to hide his own sin.

Right away God sent Nathan, His Prophet to speak with David. Nathan told David a story of a rich man who took advantage of a poor man. In the end the rich man stole the poor man's only possession (a lamb) and killed it. This infuriated King David, and he said, "As the Lord lives, the man who did this deserves to die! Because he has done this thing and shown no pity, he must pay four lambs for that lamb" (2 Sam. 12:5-6). This is when Nathan told

David that he was this man. Nathan told David all the Lord God told him to say, pointing out that God had blessed David with so much, and He would have given him more, yet he still did this and tried to hide it. God pronounced judgment on David for his actions, and, among other things, told David that his child with Bathsheba (wife of Uriah) would die. Right away David repented and asked for forgiveness, and God forgave him of his sins. However, the punishment was still going to happen. King David's son still dies after David pleaded with God to not allow it. After all this takes place, King David says this when asked by his servants about his attitude he has right after the death of his son.

> *"When David saw that his servants were whispering to each other, he guessed that the baby was dead. So he asked his servants, "Is the baby dead?" "He is dead," they replied.*
>
> *20 Then David got up from the ground. He washed, anointed himself, changed his clothes, went to the Lord's house, and worshiped. Then he went home and requested something to eat. So they served him food, and he ate. 21 His servants asked him, "What did you just do? While the baby was alive, you fasted and wept, but when he died, you got up and ate food."22 He answered, "While the baby was alive, I fasted and wept because I*

> *thought, 'Who knows? The Lord may be gracious
> to me and let him live.' 23 But now that he is dead,
> why should I fast? Can I bring him back again?
> I'll go to him, but he will never return to me." (2
> Sam. 12:19-23)*

He first repents and asks for forgiveness, and then accepts the discipline/consequence. It did not mean he could not ask God to not carry it out. We see that he did ask God not to carry out the consequence. What is important to see is his heart and attitude when it came to his consequence and how he responded to it. He had the attitude and heart of humility, faith, and assurance in the God of the Universe.

This is what God wants us to do when it comes to the entrenched sin in our lives. He wants us to know that He already knows about it. The fact is, due to His awesome gift of Jesus Christ and His sacrifice, you are already forgiven. Knowing this, we must respond in the same way King David did. We must submit to His (God's) Will, and humble ourselves to His sovereignty on our lives. We must repent, and asked for forgiveness, and for God to have mercy and take this sin from our lives; to place us on the path He has prepared for us. Our repentful heats cannot be based upon a condition either. We cannot say we are sorry and repent, "as long as you do not allow me to go through the consequences". This is not a true repentful heart. We must have the attitude of "Even if." "Even if I still must go through the consequences of my decision, I will humbly follow you, because you know best. Because you are a Just and Holy God, because you love me, and have shown mercy to me all the days of my life" Today, many believe that consequences do not apply to them. They feel, to be forgiven means nothing will happen, however, as we can see throughout scripture that is not the case at all.

Before we move on, let me once more recap our Marching Orders. First, we are told to humble ourselves, repent and ask for forgiveness (James 4:6/Acts 3:19/1 John 1:9). We may or may not have to consult or speak with someone more mature in the faith; like a Pastor or mentor in your life (like Nathan) (Matthew 18:15-17). A person that will tell you the hard truth. Then we must take whatever action is needed to make it right (Colossians 3:13/Matt. 5:23-24) and be ok with having to go through the consequence of our actions (Prov. 10:17; 12:1/Hebrews 12:10-11). Why, because we reap what we sow (Gal. 6:7-9), and God is right there with us in the hard times (Psalm 23/Heb. 13:5). The biggest thing we should take away from this is that entrenched sin will hurt you. It will continue to cause you hardship, it will cause you to lie, and avoid the truth. It will keep you from truly repenting because, avoiding it will enslave you to the guilt. Entrenched sin will hurt those around you; your actions effect everyone in your life. Your attitude, your integrity, the way your treat people are all effected by entrenched sin. Why, because of the depravity it will take to hid it, to avoid it, and to live with it. It is like mold, mold you find on a piece of bread in a loaf. If you do not cut it out, it will spread to the rest of the loaf and the whole thing will be trash.

Train How you Fight: *Here we will point out practical ways you can practice/train, so we can attempt to make these Spiritual Disciplines muscle memory.*

This Battle Drill is not something I recommend handling on your own. I recommend you work on the entrenched sin in your life with a Pastor, Spiritual Leader (Mentor), and your husband or wife. I say this because these types of sins, and issues could be deep rooted and cause many other emotions, thoughts, or memories to come up. Depending on how severe, you may also need professional Christian Counseling. Why do I say this? It is because I have had to deal with many issues/sins in my life that manifested themselves in and through my Post Traumatic Stress Disorder (PTSD), that I was diagnosed with after my first few Combat Tours. All the trauma, guilt, and sinful actions I had to face/relive caused many other emotions to surface. Without my support system (God, Pastor, mentor, and wife), I would not have made it. While I was working on these issues, I needed them to hold me accountable, encourage me, and pray for me. The method I feel worked the best when working with a support system and is very easy, and practical to do is called "Cognitive Behavior Therapy" (CBT). (Clinic, 2022) Now this method will be much more formal if you do it with a licensed Christian Counselor, however, in this chapter I will give you the gist of it. I will explain the steps and how you can use it when you meet with your Pastor or mentor, and how your spouse can help as well. Remember, I am not a licensed Counselor, and after you meet with your Pastor, the first and most important step may be to get connected with a Licensed one.

CBT is a method that helps you see and become aware of inaccurate or negative thoughts in the hopes that you will be able to view a hard memory or action clearer. The hope is that once you do this, you will react in a more effective way. This is important because sin causes guilt, and guilt causes you to have inaccurate or irrational thought about who you are and how God sees you. Therefore, we try to hide our entrenched sin, or avoid it, or justify it, because we do not want to even deal with it. But with God's help, you can have this trench entered and cleared. The first step you would work on is identifying the sin. This could be a fight, sinful anger, divorce, stealing, hurting another, greed, cheating, etc. You will have to "Say" what it is you did. This first step is in line with scripture. *"Therefore, confess your sins to one another and pray for one another, so that you may be healed. The urgent request of a righteous person is very powerful in its effect." (James 5:16).* Get it out, do not hold on to the burden by yourself.

The next step is to write down your thoughts, beliefs, and emotions about this sin. Are you telling yourself you are worthless because of this sin? Are you thinking there is no hope? Do you think God could never forgive you? Are you ashamed and feel that the person you hurt will never forgive you? How has this event changed the way you see the world, or yourself? Are you angry at yourself, or another, or at God? Be honest here, the only way to get past this part is to be honest with yourself. By writing all these thoughts or emotions down, you are now able to see them and process them (Clinic, 2022). It is amazing how writing something down and rereading it can really cause you to reevaluate or see it differently. The third step is to identify the thoughts or emotions that are unnecessarily negative, inaccurate, or irrational. For example, if you wrote down that you think that God would never forgive you. You then need to ask yourself if this thought lines up with scripture. What would help in this scenario is to look up all the scripture (which there is a lot), where God says He will forgive you. Time and time again we are told in scripture that God will forgive, and He is faithful to forgive, we just need to turn back to Him and repent (1 John 1:9; 2 Chronicles 7:14).

The last step involves taking theses inaccurate thoughts, and with the knowledge you attain showing the inaccuracy of the thoughts, you rewrite/reconstruct these inaccurate perceptions and align them to the Truth you found in the Word of God! Now the feelings and inaccurate thoughts just do not go away. We are creatures of habit as I have stated before, and we will attempt to fall back into our old thinking. This is where your support group comes in, this is where you will need your battle buddies. Once you have gone through these steps with a Counselor or Pastor, you will be able to assess the topic in your mind as it surfaces. For instance, if you are out and about, and out of nowhere the thought of a certain issue/sin comes up. It causes you start thinking how you are a failure, and that God will never forgive you. This is when you tell yourself "Stop"! "I know in the Word of God it says, *"…He is faithful and righteous to forgive us our sins""* *(1 Jn. 1:9).* You can also share with your spouse that you are having these thoughts again and they can remind you of this. This is how you put these steps into practice, and it WILL take practice. However, over time it will be come easy/second nature to do. It will happen so fast in your mind that it won't seem like a process anymore.

This is the goal of CBT. It is to help your mind and emotions create healthier patterns and create a habit of processing events and issues instead of just irrationally reacting. Now this Battle Drill is not just for the past. There could be something new you do, don't do, or are part of that will cause another "Entrenched" sin. Knowing this method, you can either write it down and discuss it with your Counselor or Pastor next time you see them. Or you can go through the steps yourself, with your Battle Buddy or Spouse in a more non-formal way. It will all depend on how comfortable you are at going through the steps, and how much you have put this into practice. Our world wants you to think you are what you do, **but I want to remind you that, you are what you have overcome through the power of Jesus Christ!**

Below I will list a great resource of connecting with Christian Councilors in your area. I keep recommending Christian Counselors because, the only way to truly heal is with God, with Christ Jesus involved. Everything the World recommends is temporary, self-centered, and will fade. The best resource is through, "The American Association of Christian Counselors" (AACC), and their site is at https://www.aacc.net/ . On their site you can become a member, learn more about them, find a counselor, or event, and other resources. Remember, sometimes it is hard to ask for help. We do not want to feel vulnerable, but the thing is, we cannot do this on our own. We need to involve God in this along with those godly people He has placed around us. It is not a fail to go see a professional, it is a win. The enemy wants you to feel ashamed to ask for help because, he knows if you don't ask it will keep you where you are at. Don't listen to the lies of the enemy. Seek God, seek help, and move forward in the power of the Holy Spirit!

Questions for thought:

1. Why do we always think the worst when we fail?

    a. Do you think we are more forgiving to other people's failures then our own? Why?

2. For those that know the truth of the Word of God. Why do we often fall victim to the lies of the enemy? (Ex. "You can never be forgiven…").

3. Why is it so hard for us to admit we need help when we were created to be in community?

    a. Do you think it has something to do with the isolation of sin? Explain.

4. Besides the method (CBT) explained in this chapter, what is another way you feel you could work through entrenched sin with God and your support system?

Chapter 9

CONDUCT INITIAL BREACH OF MINE OBSTACLE

Your Jericho

Military Explanation:

The last Battle Drill we are taught is a group drill. It is used mostly in accordance with a larger operation, and the group conducting it is just one part of this larger force. Usually, this Battle Drill is used when the larger force conducting a large operation is stopped by some sort of obstacle that is reinforced with mines/explosives. This obstacle that is encountered cannot be bypassed, and the only way around is through. What makes this a hard situation is the fact that the enemy usually knows you are there, and is attacking you from the other side while you are attempting to breach their obstacle. That being said, this battle drill has many moving parts, and is one of the hardest to become habit.

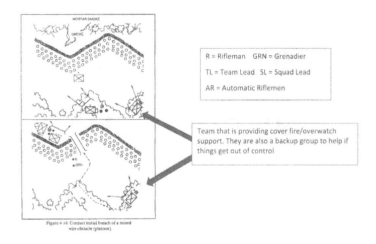

Figure 4-14. Conduct initial breach of a mined wire obstacle (platoon).

Ultimately, the platoon must set up cover fire to protect the team that will approach the obstacle. They need to gain fire superiority to keep the enemies heads down so they will not notice, or even if they notice, they won't be able to harm the team headed to the obstacle. The platoon will either call in mortar fire to send smoke, or they will deploy a smoke grenade to help conceal their movement by blinding the enemy. Once the obstacle is breached, the team will set up cover fire position on the other side. This will allow the rest of the team, squad, platoon, or company to pass through. Once they all make it though, they will continue their mission. This was a quick and brief explanation of this drill. If you want to learn more about this drill, please reference the Field Manuel 25-101 (25-101, 2022). Again, this drill is dependent on the group working together, with one goal, purpose, and as one body. You as the individual need to understand the objective, and the part you play in the whole mission/drill. This would involve you understanding what everyone else is supposed to be doing as well, just in case you have to cover down on a part that is needing help.

For this Battle Drill to be the most effective the group must be united. They must be in sync with one goal, purpose, and objective. The group must trust each other and their Commanding Officer and Sergeant. The only way to have this is to be part of a larger unit that trains together, plays together, holds each other accountable, and is there for each other during every season. There must be that assurance, that each person on the team knows what they are doing, and they will follow through no matter the circumstance. Ultimately, this is the goal with all the Battle Drills. However, this is really important for this one since it usually involves such a large group.

Biblical Parallel:

When I was pondering this battle drill, one biblical story came to mind. It was one that involved all the components of the battle drill, and it was an obstacle the People of God had to go through. They could not go around it, they could not bypass it, it had to be breached/

taken down. The biblical story I am referring to is the Battle of Jericho. This event is recorded within the first 6 chapters of the Book of Joshua. By God's grace, we get to see how they prepared, and how they carried out their mission placed before them by God. Now I will be briefly going through the main points of the story, and because of that I encourage you to read this portion of scripture in its entirety on your own.

The book of Joshua opens with an encouraging word from God. A promise that God would be with them, go before them, and He would be their strength and courage. Next, we see Joshua preparing the people to move across the Jordan, to move forward with the mission God gave to them. Next, they did a little reconnaissance of the area, the first city, and the terrain. Now everything their parents saw was still there. The city was a fertile land, and there were still large people living there, and it was something any Nation would desire. The difference is they (this next generation), was united in the goal. They all understood what God had promised them, and they trusted each other, but most of all they trusted God. This new generation also remembered the distrust and disobedience their Parents were involved in when Moses tried to lead them into the Promise Land right after their exodus from Egypt. Therefore, instead of delivering a report that caused fear and doubt, they reported one of encouragement and assurance (Joshua 2:24). Then they moved forward with the mission at hand. They stepped out in faith even though they did not yet have a battle plan. They had faith in what they were told by Joshua from God, that He has already defeated their enemies, they just had to get there. In Chapter 5, Joshua had to ensure all the people of Israel were circumcised according to their covenant. None of this generation was circumcised due to the dis-obedience of their Parents whom God saved from Egypt. Joshua had to ensure all this generation was right before God, obediently following their covenant promise before expecting the Blessing (a mistake their parents made). Not too long after this, Joshua encounters the "Commander of the Lord's Army" (5:13-15). This is where God instructs Joshua on what to do.

Joshua is told by God to gather the fighting Men of Israel, the Ark, and the Priests. They were to march around the city one time each day for six days with the Ark. The Priests were instructed to blow the trumpets during their march around the city each time, and during these six days the people must not say a word or make a sound. The seventh day would be different than the rest. On the seventh day, they are to march around the city seven times. When they complete the seventh circle around the city, the Priests are to make a prolonged trumpet sound, and all the men are to shout. After they shout, God would give them their victory. This is exactly what happened, the walls came down, and they were able to victoriously enter the city (Due to their unity, trust in God, and obedience). They were trumpet in their breach of this first obstacle of their mission for the Promise Land. What a powerful story of unity, purpose, goal, assurance, and faith! The story of Jericho displays the same level of operation at hand for this drill. The battle drill we are discussing is usually part of a larger operation. This battle was the beginning of the larger conquest of the Promise Land. The battle drill involves trust, unity, and purpose; a reason for the soldiers to come together and fight as one. The Battle of Jericho has these same elements; however, they are all tied into God and His Will.

What does this mirror in our lives? Those situations that we must confront or get right before God before we can move forward in our walk with Him. This could be reconciliation with a brother or sister in Christ. It could be reconciliation with a stranger or acquaintance. It could be a situation that involves you asking for forgiveness or forgiving another. It could be getting over your pride and following through with what God has placed before you. A great story to read regarding this type of pride can be found in 2 Kings 5, the story of Naaman. For anyone that is recovering from addiction, it could be seeking out those you have hurt while in your addiction. Whatever it may be, there are situations in our lives that become obstacles in our walk. The only way to grow and move forward is to "Breach" them. There are also things God asks us to do that seem like obstacles. For example, God may want you to pray with someone you have just met on the street. The obstacle may be nerves, or fear, or pride. Can you get over it, will you "Breach" these obstacles to do as God has asked? Maybe it is leaving your current job to do ministry, or sell your favorite possession to help a hurting family member or friend. Whatever it is, there is usually an obstacle in the way trying to deter us, to discourage us from doing what God has asked us to do. The problem with not following through with what God has asked is, you will become like the generation that died in the wilderness for lack of faith instead of entering the Promise Land (Numbers 13:25-14:10/Deut. 1:35-36). The biggest spiritual discipline we see here is faith and trust, which go hand in hand. God has promised to go before us, He has promised to fight for us, He has promised us victory. But it will not happen if we just give up, and bunker down on the wrong side of the Obstacle in our lives.

Our Marching Orders:

The Bible yet again is very clear when it comes to what we are to do in situations such as this. There are many stories to choose from, and I will speak on a few. The first one I will talk about that teaches us our Marching Orders can be found in Genesis. The story of Abraham being tested by God, and being asked to sacrifice the promise, his son Isaac (Gen 22). I would recommend you read this whole story if you have not done so before. I will just be hitting on the Spiritual Disciplines we are to get from this story. One disclaimer, these Spiritual Disciplines are not the only things you can learn from this story. Our God's Word is alive, and there is no way for us to get it all from one reading of the passage. This goes for all the stories I have shared and will share. So, the two Spiritual Disciplines I want to point out are Faith, and Trust (which really go hand in hand). In this story, God asks Abraham to sacrifice his son, the son of the promise God made with him back in Genesis 12 and 15 (to name a few chapters). What we see is God wanting to know if Abraham has faith, and trusts Him. We see earlier in this story starting in chapter 12, all the way up to 22, Abraham seems to have a faith and trust issue.

In chapter 12 around verse 10, Abram is fearful of his life due to the beauty of his wife Sarai and asks her to pretend she is his sister. Why do this? Does he not think God will protect them when it was God that asked him to leave his home and family? In the next few chapters, we see his attitude change. We see him trust God when separating with his nephew Lot (Chapter 13), when he goes to war to rescue Lot (chapter 14), and when God reassures him of the promise in Chapter 15. Once we get into Chapter 16, we see some doubt creep in. Due to Sarai not having any children yet, they turn to their Egyptian servant girl. Abram sleeps with her, and she conceives Ishmael. This decision based on their doubt caused issues for his decedents which are still occurring today (division and fighting between Muslims and Israel). In Chapter 18 Sarai, now Sarah, laughs at the announcement that she will indeed have a child that she will conceive. And once more in chapter 20, Abraham is fearful of his life and lies about his wife Sarah, saying she is his sister. This lie almost caused the death of someone unaware of the treachery (Gen 20:3-10). Finally, in chapter 21, the promise is born.

As we can see, there has been champion moments for Abraham and Sarah, and there have been low moments. There is an obstacle here that God wants Abraham to "Breach" and get past. For Abraham to be who he is supposed to be, he must get past the fear and doubt. We know he has faith, and we know he trusts God, but there are defining moments where he allowed fear and doubt to become an obstacle that caused issues for him and his walk with God. Faith and Trust can only be demonstrated in action. Therefore, it was not enough for him to say or think that all will be just fine. We are alluded to this attitude of faith and trust in his remarks in Gen 22:7-8, where Isaac asks where the sacrifice is, and Abraham says that God will provide. It is even alluded in verse 5 where he tells the servants that *"we'll come back to you"*, showing he trusted they would both return. This attitude was just the start, it is where the faith and trust begin, but there must be action, or it is just words. Think about trust falls. The action where someone will fall backwards, trusting that the other person participating will catch them. They can say all day that they trust and have faith that the other person will catch them. It is totally different when they must actually do something that places their safety in the other persons hands and fall backwards.

Abraham is about to sacrifice his son, the promise, when God steps in and stops him. Then God says, *""Do not lay a hand on the boy or do anything to him. For now I know that you fear God, since you have not withheld your only son from Me"* (Gen 22:12). Because Abraham trusted God and had faith, he was able to "Breach the Obstacle" in his life. Causing him to be the champion of the faith we hear so much about in scripture (Matthew 1:1-2; 3:9; 8:11; 22:32; Mark 12:26; Luke 1:55; 1:73; 3:8; 3:34; 13:16, 28; 16:23-30; 19:9; 20:37; John 8:39, 40, 52-58), several times in Acts (3:13,25; 7:2-32; 13:26) and Hebrews (6:13,15; 7:1-10; 11:8-12; 17-19) as well as in James (2:21-23) and once in 1 Peter (3:6) . Faith and Trust, things we must have in order to please God, and to be able to allow God to mold us through Christ, into who we were created to be.

Another great story in the Bible that shows us what we are to do with the Obstacles we are faced with in life, in our walk with Christ, is found in the book of Daniel. The story of Shadrach, Meshach, and Abednego found in Daniel 3. Again, I will just be highlighting portions of this story. I encourage you to read the whole thing, as this is another rich story that has many things to gain from reading it. In this story we are told of three Jews that were in captivity. These famous names we know are the names the King of Babylon gave to them. Before they were taken with Daniel into captivity, their Hebrew names were

Hananiah (changed to Shadrach), Mishael (changed to Meshach), and Azariah (changed to Abednego) (Daniel 1:7b). In chapter 3 they are faced with an obstacle. The King decides to build a huge statue and tells all the land that they will bow down and worship it when they hear the sound of the musical instruments (Daniel 3:4). It was already told to the people of the land that if they did not bow down, they would be thrown into the Fiery furnace (Dan. 3:6). If their whole situation was not bad enough. They (Shadrach, Meshach, and Abednego) already were taken from their home, their names stripped from them, and now they were being told to worship an Idol. What an obstacle… what would they do? Would they avoid it (give in)? Would they pretend (justify their actions… "I was just pretending to worship…")?

No, what we see is they do not bow down to worship it. When the music plays, everyone around them bows down except for them. The King is informed and gets so upset he has the furnace kindled to the hottest it can be (Dan. 3:19). The King gives them one more chance to bow down, and they answer the King by saying. *"Shadrach, Meshach, and Abednego replied to the king, "Nebuchadnezzar, we don't need to give you an answer to this question. If the God we serve exists, then He can rescue us from the furnace of blazing fire, and He can rescue us from the power of you, the king. But even if He does not rescue us, we want you as king to know that we will not serve your gods or worship the gold statue you set up (Dan 3:16-18)."* So, long story short. They are thrown in, but they are not harmed. From what we are told, the King saw another standing in there with them that looked like the son of gods (Dan. 3:26). When the King orders them to be released, only the three of them came out. They were not burned, scorched, nor did they smell like fire or smoke. After this the King made a proclamation honoring Yahweh, and he rewarded Shadrach, Meshach, and Abednego (Dan. 3:29-30).

What do we learn from this story of the Fiery Furnace? Not only do we see that they had faith and trust in Yahweh. They also desired to honor God in word and deed so much, they cared for His glory above their own (even above their own safety). Now, I am not necessarily telling you to go get thrown into a fiery furnace. What I am trying to show you is the only way to make it past certain obstacles in your walk, not only takes faith and trust, but it also takes a heart for God. A heart for God that cares for His glory, His Will to be done, His Name to be known throughout all the Nations. This desire realizes that you are part of a bigger mission, and the fact remains that if you have Christ you are going to be ok no matter what (you have your salvation). But there are those that do not know Him, and the <u>only way for them to know Him is for you to Breach that obstacle.</u> Then we (the Church), can continue the mission of winning souls for Christ. Just look at the evidence in the Bible. Every time someone trusted and had faith as they allowed God to lead them through an obstacle, His name was glorified and they were remembered as examples for us, Champions of the faith.

This Battle Drill involves a mature believer, or one that has a great support group/battle buddies that know what they are doing. This battle drill involves many elements of all the other drills. It involved someone that has a deep relationship with God, one that is bathed in prayer, founded in Scripture, and supported by other soldiers of the Church. Again, talk is cheap when it comes to saying you have faith and trust. It is another thing to walk into a furnace to tell the world that your God and His Will is worth dying for! What Obstacle have you been avoiding? What do you need to breach to further your walk?

Train How you Fight: *Here we will point out practical ways you can practice/train, so we can attempt to make these Spiritual Disciplines muscle memory.*

This Battle Drill took me a while to figure out a practical way to "Practice" it. I mean, how do you "Train How you Fight" an obstacle, unless there is really one there? After much prayer and talking with others more mature in the faith (believers). I have found one way to do this. You got to start small! Faith and trust are grown when used. Therefore, you see so many biblical characters putting their faith and trust in action. To start small means to pick an obstacle in your life that is not a huge issue to start with/to practice with. For example, cursing. For many, this is not that big of a deal to stop doing. First, you must go to God in prayer for guidance, wisdom, and determination to breach this obstacle. Then each day you make an intentional decision to not use specific words (Curse words). You trust God to give you strength, and you have faith He will get you through. You will also want to ensure you tell your Battle Buddies about your decision, so they can encourage you and hold you accountable also. Then when a moment comes when you want to curse, you make a conscious decision to bite your tongue and glorify God over getting even with someone with words.

This same concept works with the obstacle of changing your diet or becoming more physically active to become healthier. You plan to go to the gym once a week, you put it on your calendar, and create a reminder. You need to tell someone of this decision to help encourage you and hold you accountable. Then, once you breach this obstacle (you start to make it to the gym at least once a week), you up the ante to two or three times. It becomes easier and easier to get yourself to go, and you become healthier, which will prosper you (longer life, etc..). With a diet, you start somewhere also (Start Small). For example, you stop drinking soda first, then you cut out fast food maybe. The point again is starting small but starting somewhere, and putting these little goals into practice which become easier and easier to accomplish when you carry them out with accountability. Starting small is exactly what we see the biblical authors sharing with us when they recorded certain events where they (or the person/people they wrote about), breach obstacles in their walk with God.

Remember the story of Shadrach, Meshach, and Abednego? What about Daniel and the Lion's den? How did they get to the point where they could face an obstacle that severe/big? To find out, all we must do is dive into scripture in Daniel 1 and 2. In chapter 1, Daniel and his three friends are faced with a small obstacle when first taken into captivity. They are told they will be required to eat food that is against their food laws that God gave them. Now they could have been like everyone else and ate, then justified it later, thus avoiding the obstacle that would give them issues in the future. "I am in captivity, God will understand. He does not want me to die right…" However, they trusted, had faith, and desired to honor God so much so they took a risk (as they could be punished for not eating what the King gave them). Starting small for them was asking the servant placed in charge of their care to allow them to eat vegetables for 10 days with water. If they looked sick or worse off than all the others, then they would eat the Kings food. Seems simple right? This is what Scripture tells us happened because of this faith in action, and trust in God.

> *15 "At the end of 10 days they looked better and healthier than all the young men who were eating the king's food. 16 So the guard continued*

to remove their food and the wine they were to drink and gave them vegetables. 17 God gave these four young men knowledge and understanding in every kind of literature and wisdom. Daniel also understood visions and dreams of every kind. 18 At the end of the time that the king had said to present them, the chief official presented them to Nebuchadnezzar. 19 The king interviewed them, and among all of them, no one was found equal to Daniel, Hananiah, Mishael, and Azariah. So they began to serve in the king's court. 20 In every matter of wisdom and understanding that the king consulted them about, he found them times better than all the diviner-priests and mediums in his entire kingdom." Daniel 1:15-20 (HCSB)

They started small, and they trusted and had faith in God to care for them and help them through this obstacle. Because of this faithfulness, they prospered, God blessed them, and they grew in faith and righteousness. In chapter 2, they are faced with another obstacle. This one is a bit bigger and more serious than the one we just spoke about. This is when the King had a dream and was troubled by it, and asked for his wisemen to tell him the dream and explain it. No one could do it, and they all were facing death because they displeased the King. Daniel and his three friends faced this obstacle courageously, and boldly. They came to God asking Him to reveal the dream and meaning to them. Their faith and trust grew from the first time, and now they applied it again. God revealed the dream and meaning to them, and Daniel informed the King giving all credit to Yahweh (Dan. 2:27-30). The King was so pleased that he again gave glory to Yahweh himself, and he again gave rewards to Daniel and his three friends.

> *46 "Then King Nebuchadnezzar fell down, paid homage to Daniel, and gave orders to present an offering and incense to him. 47 The king said to Daniel, "Your God is indeed God of gods, Lord of kings, and a revealer of mysteries, since you were able to reveal this mystery." 48 Then the king promoted Daniel and gave him many generous gifts. He made him ruler over the entire province of Babylon and chief governor over all the wise men of Babylon. 49 At Daniel's request, the king appointed Shadrach, Meshach, and Abednego to manage the province of Babylon. But Daniel remained at the king's court." Dan. 2:46-49 (HCSB)*

To train how you fight for this Battle Drill involves starting small. I really cannot say exactly what to do, as "something small" will look different for everyone. We see in the stories shared that starting small is the best way to go. Start with an obstacle that does not seem like that big a deal for you. Go to God in prayer, and guidance. Then move forward in faith, trusting that God will get you through. This will not only grow your faith and trust, but it will also move the Will of God forward, help the larger mission at hand (making disciples of all nations), and you will be blessed. Remember, you do not want to start with a big obstacle like a fiery furnace when you can start small. Training how you fight, creates that muscle memory that becomes habit to react in righteousness, and the ability to breach these obstacles with trust and faith in a God that will never let you down. We have story after story, testimony after testimony telling us this is the way!

Questions for thought:

1. What obstacle/s are you facing currently in your life or Spiritual Journey?

    a. Would you consider them small ones or large?

2. After reading all these biblical examples, what does "Starting Small" look like for you?

3. How you Breached an Obstacle in your walk before? How did you make it through?

    a.   Did you get to see God glorified through it all as we see in Daniel when the Kings gives glory to God? If so, how?

4.   Why do we find it so hard to trust God when He has never let us down?

    a.   Do you have an example of when you did and when you didn't? How did each turn out?

Chapter 10

REFLECTION

Review

What do Battle Drills teach us? For those that have never heard the word "Battle Drill" or have never heard the concept of this type of training, I hope you have walked away with at least a small understanding. To sum up the book, and to answer this question, let me explain. Battle Drills teach us repetition. It is a practical way to teach and train your body to make a decision and/or react a certain way with little to no thought. Throughout this book I have given many examples of practical ways followers of Christ can implement activities/actions they can practice, creating this type of muscle memory. These examples I have given are not the only ones that can be used, there are many other ways to do so. It would come down to you, who you have as support around you (Battle Buddies), where you live, your resources, and time that you have to practice.

You may think this whole concept is too simple, and it would not work. The fact remains that God created us as creatures of habit in a manner of speaking. The

Bible does not specifically state this, but we can see that we are from observation. We get in our routine and react a certain way consistently throughout our lives. Many times, we do not stray from these habits/routines until they are pointed out to us. Usually, they are pointed out to us because these are the "bad habits" we practice. It could be picking your nose, twirling your hair, picking your teeth after you eat, the order you get ready in the morning, or even your eating habits. These habits and routines are even found in our mental health. An example of this would be, if you are raised in an environment that has consistent yelling or condemning. Your habit is to become defensive right away when confronted for anything, and it would result in you yelling back, or shutting down in all probability.

Another example I can share to drive this point home has to do with me. When I was struggling with Alcoholism, I had created bad habits regarding this issue. To cope with mental health issues, I had received from physical and mental trauma from my combat deployments. I would drink to feel better and forget. It was not a habit at first, but when I felt the temporary relief, I kept practicing this action for the temporary result. Soon, it became natural for me to go straight for a bottle of alcohol when my feelings or memories overwhelmed me. I did not even have to think about it, I would get home and go straight to the fridge. It was not until my problem was pointed out to me multiple times that I realized I had to change. By then

I hit rock bottom, and that made me realize I needed to turn back to God. So, I rededicated my life to Christ, and made a consciences decision to change this habit (with the guidance of the Holy Spirit); that is when change started. When the memories came, or the feels flooded my being, I had to fight the battle within that wanted to go back to the bad/old habits. I had to prayerfully practice the new habits, the ones that align with Scripture, with God, and the purpose He has for my life. I had to set up practical ways to help me see when to put these new habits into action (having someone with me, ensuring I did not go anywhere that had alcohol, etc.). Even having someone to call if I felt I was about to give in, so I could be talked down. Now I am at a point where many of these actions are habit. I react in ways that help me stay away from drinking altogether. Due to these new habits, and God's grace, I have been sober for over 10 years. This concept works, we are creatures of habit, and creating new ones is a tried-and-true way to help you change your life for the better (always with God leading the way).

Why It Relates to the Bible

In the Bible we are told to love our enemies (Matt. 5:42-44), to go and sin no more (John 8:11), to be holy as our God is (1 Peter 1:15), and to have the mind of Christ (Phil 2:4). These are all actions we must choose to implement. They are also actions that will take deliberate and concise decisions to do when faced with what the world will through at you. God asks us to choose between what the world would want us to do, and what He not only wants us to do, but what He created us for. Our amazing God has given us the tools we need, He has laid it all out in Scripture, He has walked this earth and showed us (Jesus). Now we are to work out our Salvation in this way. Not that you can earn your Salvation, no, that is not what I am saying. When Paul says,

> *"12 So then, my dear friends, just as you have always obeyed, not only in my presence, but now even more in my absence, work out your own salvation with fear and trembling. 13 For it is God who is working in you, enabling you both to desire and to work out His good purpose." (Phil. 2:12-13 HCSB)*

What Paul is saying is we must put into practice what God has asked of us. We need to allow Him to work in us and through us according to His Will and purpose. Everything the Bible reveals to us to do, is something that will take practice for lack of a better term. It is like working out at the gym. The more you go and workout, the stronger you get, and the healthier you get. The same goes for our walk with Christ. The more we practice what He taught, the stronger our faith grows, the stronger our Christlikeness becomes. The Battle Drill technique I have shared do just this. It was created to make a regular person into a more proficient soldier. So, to take this technique, and apply it to our spiritual life, it would help create a stronger/more proficient follower of Christ. Of course, you would have to be aware of the danger of it meaning nothing if your heart did not change with your action (you would just be going through the motions). Therefore, keeping Christ at the center of all of this, and seeking Him and His Will in it all, protects/guards your heart from that danger.

Talk is Cheap

Talking about it, reading it, or arguing over how to do it is cheap. Action speaks louder than words. This is so true when it comes to your walk with Christ. You can say all day you know what to do, that you want to be better, that you want to live Christ-like, but what you do says more than your words. The only way to become a better runner is to run. The only way to become a better athlete is to practice. The only way to be a better public speaker is to speak publicly. Many things in life only get better when we practice, when we put in the effort to be better at whatever it is. The same goes with our walk with Christ. James says it the best I think when he says, *"22 But be doers of the word and not hearers only, deceiving yourselves." (James 1:22)*

Make it Your Own

It is important that you make it your own. You do not have to use my ideas as an "only choice". This book is just supposed to spark ideas in your heart on how you can grow closer, deeper, and humbly with Jesus Christ. The goal is to have you understand the concept I have described throughout this book about "Battle Drills", so you can learn to live in a way where you react in righteousness, not sin. So prayerfully seek a way that you can use what you have learned to grow. Remember to keep it simple, we do not need to give ourselves more work, life is hard enough. An important thing I want to reiterate is having a "Battle Buddy". Someone that will look out for you, rebuke you, encourage you, and have your back. We were created to be in community, and the Bible is clear that we are stronger together.

> *11 Also, if two lie down together, they can keep warm; but how can one person alone keep warm? 12 And if someone overpowers one person, two can resist him. A cord of three strands is not easily broken. 13 Better is a poor but wise youth than an old but foolish king who no longer pays attention to warnings. (Ecclesiastes 4:11-13).*

Again, the goal is to surround yourself with people that will help you grow in Christ, and to find ways you can practice reacting righteously, glorifying God, and not reacting in a sinful way. Make it your own. Make it work in your context and circumstance, and trust that God is with you all the way.

Nothing Replaces the Bible

Another goal of mine with this book was to point you to the Bible. In no way do I think I have all the answers, or that my ideas trump scripture. The Bible is our foundation, it is our measuring stick for life. The Scriptures of the Old and New Testaments were given by inspiration of God, and they only constitute the divine rule for Christian faith and practice. To help you find ways to practice your battle drills, you must read the Bible. You must read it, study it, apply it, ponder it, and then live it out. But most of all, share it with others too. The other part of this is prayer. If you are reading the Bible, but you are not talking to the one that gave it to you (God), what good will it do? The Bible is here to reveal who God is, what He has done, is doing, and will do for His creation. It was given to help us, and to guide us in a relationship with Him. However, if you do not communicate with Him, is there a relationship? There cannot be a true relationship with anyone without communication… So, pray!

You Will Always be a Disciple

What is a Disciple? The definition is a student of a teacher, leader, or philosopher. In the context of the Bible, it is someone that is personally following Jesus Christ. As long as Jesus is your Lord and Savior, you will always be a Disciple. You will always be a student, learning, growing, and maturing (becoming more Christ-like). If you do not think of yourself as a Disciple, you will not grow. When you are not a student you do not care to learn, you do not care to seek and gain more knowledge. However, if you have the mind of a Disciple, a student, you will keep coming back for more. You will come to the Bible for answers, then get you answer, but walk away with more questions. This will be your cycle, one that will help you continue to grow into the person God created you to be. It is like an athlete trying new ways and techniques to be better at his game, to stay relevant and the best in the game. This is paramount.

The next step in living out a life of a Disciple is to Disciple others. You cannot be a Disciple if you do not make more (Disciple others). Matthew 28:19-20 (HCSB), *"**Go, therefore**, and make disciples of all nations, baptizing them in the name of the Father and of the Son and of the Holy Spirit, **teaching them to observe everything I have commanded you**. And remember, I am with you always, to the end of the age." (Bold font for emphasis).* Teaching others and learning yourself go hand in hand here. Christ has "sent" us; He has given us the green light. We are to learn and grow all our lives, reflecting His glory, as well as making more/multiplying ourselves for the Kingdom of God. Be someone's Battle Buddy, help another grow as you did. Be a Paul to someone, but never stop being a Timothy as you grow into the Man or Women of God you were created to be.

Share the Gospel, tell others of the goodness of God. Share the news of the cross, of His redemption, His sacrifice for us all. Teach them to read the Bible, to pray, to seek the Kingdom of God first and foremost. Share His mercy, grace, and forgiveness to a world that desperately needs its... and when necessary, use words.

There is a war raging around us, are you prepared to fight?

> *May the Lord, my rock, be praised, who trains my hands for battle and my fingers for warfare. 2 He is my faithful love and my fortress, my stronghold and my deliverer. He is my shield, and I take refuge in Him; He subdues my people under me."*
> *(Psalms 144:1-2)*

Chapter 11

SUPPORT THE MINISTRY

Participate in this Ministry

Thank you for taking the time to read this book, "Soldiers and Their Battle Drills", either on your own, or with a group. It is my prayer that God has touched your heart in a way that will stir it into action in the Kingdom. I pray that it has opened your eyes to ways you can create muscle memory and habits that will honor God and help you grow and mature in Christ. Remember, who should you or I fear when we have Christ as Lord? Our reward is in heaven, our assurance is with Him who sits at the right side of the Father, and our forgiveness is proven with the empty tomb!

If you were blessed by the reading of this book, I would ask that you help me with three things that you can do that would greatly help this ministry God has placed on my heart. 1) please share and recommend this book to your family, friends, and acquaintances. 2) If God has put it in your heart, please consider donating to the ministry. There are many sacrifices in writing a book, and we cannot do it without your support. When you support the Kingdom of God with your donations/offerings you become co-laborers with Christ and all those involved in the ministry. Participate in the harvest. Jesus said in Matthew 9:37, *"Then He said to His disciples, "The harvest is abundant, but the workers are few."* 3) Consider following me on social media. You can find me on Facebook, Instagram, and YouTube when you search Pastor Jesse Posner.

If you would like to support the ministry with a donation, please email me at **jesse_posner@yahoo.com**, or find me on Venmo at **@jesse_posner**

Thank you and may God bless you,
your family, and
all those around you!

About The Author

I was born and raised in Southern California in a Christian home. Growing up I knew who Jesus was, and I was told what He did for me and all creation. I was taught of His love, and how to live a life that reflects His love and forgiveness. However, like a lot of teens, I rebelled from what I was taught, and believed that I knew best. Due to that decision, I started down a path that led to addiction, drug abuse, and fornication. This spiritual battle for my soul raged on and continued throughout High School. After High School, I joined the United States Army thinking that would help me. Now the Military did help me in many ways, but not in the way I thought it would when it came to my struggle with substance abuse. The Military taught me many necessary lessons, and disciplines, however, it was not enough to equip me in the Spiritual War raging around me 24 hours a day. I was in the Military for 13 years, and due to the physical and mental trauma I received from my three (3) combat tours, I abused alcohol and drugs to forget and dull the pain. This abuse overtook me, and because of it I almost lost my family. At that moment, the moment where I almost lost my family, I finally went to get help.

While in a Military rehab, I rededicated my life to Christ (Feb 2012), and have been serving Him ever since.

If I had seen life the way I see it now, maybe, just maybe things would have been different. Looking back, I do not wish I could change what I did and what I went through necessarily. I know that God allowed me to go through all of it to mold me into who He needs me to be in His Kingdom. To be able to bring more to the saving knowledge of Jesus Christ with the guidance and direction of the Holy Spirit. Long story short, because of the grace of God on my life, I was able to save my marriage. I am still married to Aline, I have two amazing girls (Kailynn and Audrey), and we love Christ Jesus with all our being. God has truly blessed me. My hope is to equip Christians young and old, veteran, and new, for the battle raging on around us all. To truly see the world as it is…a battlefield! This way they will be more prepared than I was. Thank you, God, for your love and forgiveness. Thank you, Jesus, for your free gift of Salvation through your Sacrifice, and for leading by example; and thank you to all my family and loved ones (especially Aline my wife) that has stood by me though all the hardship and trials.

> *This book is dedicated to God, and all Glory due to Him. It is also dedicated to Aline, Kailynn, and Audrey. May the God of Heaven and the Earth bless them all the days of their lives!

Bibliography

25-101, F., 2022. Chapter 4 - BATTLE DRILLS - FM 7-8 Infantry Rifle Platoon and Squad. [online] 550cord.com. Available at: <https://550cord.com/infantry-rifle-platoon-squad-fm-7-8/fm-7-8-chapter-4-battle-drills [Accessed 20 April 2022].

Clinic, M., 2022. Cognitive behavioral therapy - Mayo Clinic. [online] Mayoclinic.org. Available at: <https://www.mayoclinic.org/tests-procedures/cognitive-behavioral-therapy/about/pac-20384610> [Accessed 20 April 2022].

Hibbard, F. and Whedon, D., 1909. The Book of Psalms. New York: Eaton & Mains.

Appendix A

Passages Quoted or Referenced By Chapter

Chapter 1

Ephesians 6:10-20
1 John 1:8

Chapter 2

Genesis 3
Isaiah 14:12-15
1 John 5:19
1 Peter 5:8
John 8:44
Genesis 12:2-3
Matthew 28:16-20
1 Corinthians 13; 1 John 4:7-8; 1 Peter 4:8
Acts 28:31; 1 Peter 3:15
Matthew 5:16; Micah 6:8
James 1:22
Ecclesiastes 4:11-13
Luke 12:11-12

Chapter 3

Matthew 4:1-11
Matthew 4:4
1 Peter 5:8; John 10:10; Ephesians 6:11
1 Corinthians 10:13
Matthew 26:41
Ecclesiastes 4:11-13
Hebrews 10:19-25

Chapter 4

1 Corinthians 6:18
1 Timothy 6:9-11
2 Timothy 2:22
1 Timothy 6:13
1 Corinthians 10:31-33
Genesis 39:11-13
Proverbs 3:5; 1 Cor. 10:13
Proverbs 6:18
Matthew 4
1 Corinthians 10:13

Chapter 5

Joshua 8:1-24; Judges 9:31-40; 2 Samuel 3:27; 5:23-25
1 Peter 5:8-9
Genesis 27:5

Matthew 22:15-17
1 Peter 5:8-9
John 10:10
Colossians 3:1
Psalm 56:3
Matthew 28:20
Hebrews 13:4-6
Psalm 56:4;10
Matthew 10:28
James 4:7
Psalm 56:7; 11-12
Psalm 103:8
Romans 12:19; Deuteronomy 32:35
Matthew 5:43-48

Chapter 6

John 5
Romans 7:15-20
Romans 7:24-25
Matthew 16:24-26
2 Corinthians 5:17
Romans 7:15-20
Philippians 2:1-4
2 Timothy 3:16; Romans 15:2
John 15:5-7
Genesis 1:27-28
2 Peter 3:9

Proverbs 16:18
James 4:6
James 4:10

Chapter 7

2 Corinthians 5:17
Mark 16:16; Romans 10:9; 1 John 5:4; John 3:16-17
Philippians 3:15-17 (Referencing the first 3 chapters)
Psalm 139:23-24
Psalms 139:1-2
Psalms 139:7-10
1 Corinthians 4:16-17
1 Corinthians 11:1

Chapter 8

Isaiah 6:4
Isaiah 6:5-6
1 John 1:9
Isaiah 53:11; Hebrews 9
Joshua 6:15- Ch 7.
Ecclesiastes 12:14
2 Samuel Ch. 11-12
2 Samuel 12:5-6
2 Samuel 12:19-23
James 4:6/Acts 3:19/1 John 1:9
Matthew 18:15-17

Colossians 3:13/Matthew 5:23-24
Proverbs 10:17; 12:1/Hebrews 12:10-11
Galatians 6:7-9
Psalm 23/Heb. 13:5
James 5:16
1 John. 1:9

Chapter 9

Joshua Ch. 1-6
Joshua 2:24
Joshua 5:13-15
2 Kings 5
Numbers 13:25-14:10/Deuteronomy 1:35-36
Genesis 22
Genesis 12, and 15
Genesis 13, 14, 15, and 16
Genesis 18
Genesis 20:3-10 and Ch. 21
Genesis 22:7-8
Matthew 1:1-2; 3:9; 8:11; 22:32
Mark 12:26
Luke 1:55; 1:73; 3:8; 3:34; 13:16, 28; 16:23-30; 19:9; 20:37
John 8:39, 40, 52-58
Acts 3:13,25; 7:2-32; 13:26
Hebrews 6:13,15; 7:1-10; 11:8-12; 17-19
James 2:21-23
1 Peter 3:6

Daniel 3
Daniel 1-2

Chapter 10

Matthew 5:42-44
John 8:11
1 Peter 1:15
Philippians 2:4
Philippians 2:12-13
James 1:22
Ecclesiastes 4:11-13
Matthew 28:19-20
Psalms 144:1-2

Chapter 11

Matthew 9:37

CPSIA information can be obtained
at www.ICGtesting.com
Printed in the USA
BVHW032201160822
644776BV00013B/452

9 781662 852398